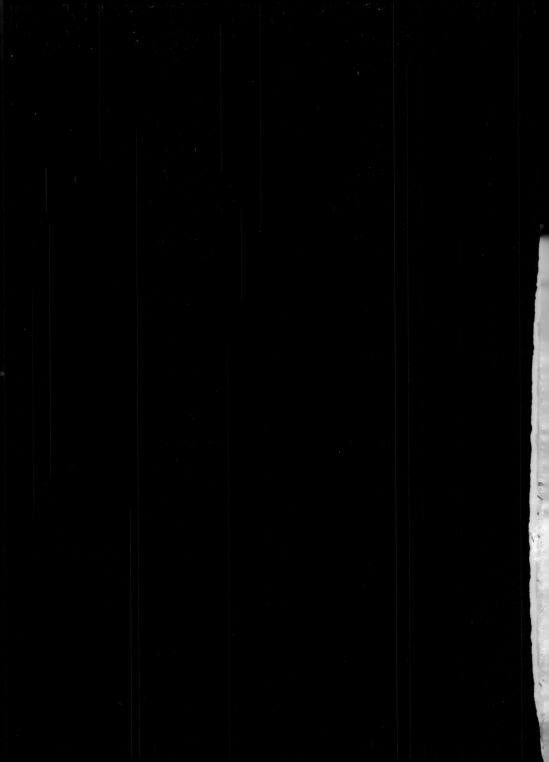

WEIRD WEATHER

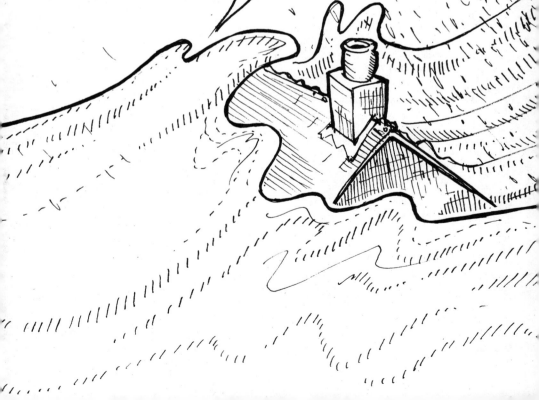

Groundwood Books / House of Anansi Press
110 Spadina Avenue, Suite 801
Toronto, Ontario M5V 2K4
Distributed in the USA by Publishers Group West
1700 Fourth Street, Berkeley, CA 94710

We acknowledge for their financial support of our
publishing program the Canada Council for the Arts,
the Government of Canada through the Book Publishing Industry Development Program (BPIDP) and the
Ontario Arts Council.

ONTARIO ARTS COUNCIL
CONSEIL DES ARTS DE L'ONTARIO

Library and Archives Canada
Cataloguing in Publication
Evans, Kate
Weird weather : everything you didn't want to know
about climate change but probably should find out
/ by Kate Evans ; with an introduction by George
Monbiot.
Includes bibliographical references.
ISBN-13: 978-0-88899-838-5 (bound)
ISBN-10: 0-88899-838-4 (bound)
ISBN-13: 978-0-88899-841-5 (pbk.)
ISBN-10: 0-88899-841-4 (pbk.)
1. Climatic changes–Juvenile literature. 2. Global
warming–Juvenile literature. I. Title.
QC981.8.C5W34 2007 j363.738'74 C2007-900289-7

This book is printed on Rolland Enviro paper: it
contains 100% post-consumer recycled fibers, is
acid-free and is processed chlorine-free.

Printed and bound in Canada

Weird weather we're having at the moment, isn't it, dear?

Everything you *didn't* want to know about climate change, but probably should find out.

BY KATE EVANS

GROUNDWOOD BOOKS
HOUSE OF ANANSI PRESS
TORONTO   BERKELEY

"THIS CARTOON WILL GET UNDER YOUR DEFENCES." MAYER HILLMAN AUTHOR OF HOW WE CAN SAVE THE PLANET

"IT'S REALLY FUNNY." MARK MASLIN, AUTHOR OF GLOBAL WARMING: A VERY SHORT INTRODUCTION

"IT GETS THE POINT ACROSS LIKE A SIX INCH NAIL HIT WITH A SLEDGEHAMMER." COLIN FORREST, CLIMATE SCIENTIST

"A BRILLIANT RESOURCE!" DR. CLARE SAUNDERS, UNIVERSITY OF KENT

CONTENTS

THERE ARE ALSO **SCIENTIFIC REFERENCES**
AT THE END OF EACH CHAPTER, ON PAGES **39, 58,
70** AND **89** RESPECTIVELY. SOME OF THESE PROVIDE
A CONTEXT TO THE CARTOON, SO CHECK THEM OUT.

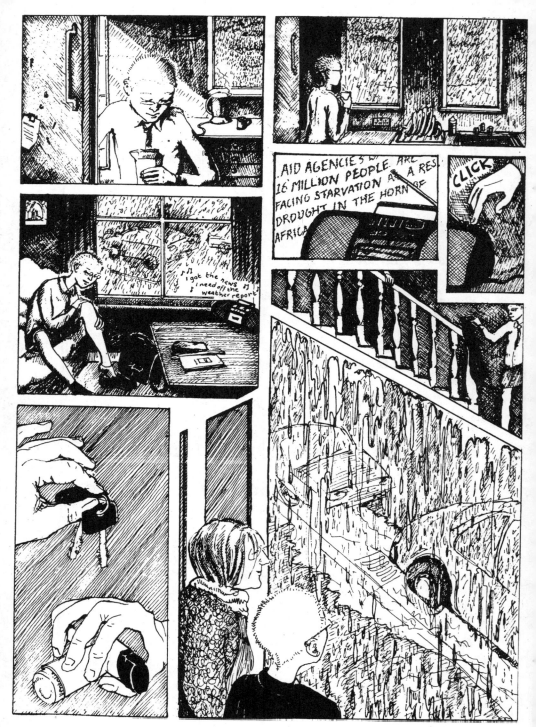

INTRODUCTION BY GEORGE MONBIOT

I think there are two reasons why climate change isn't yet the world's biggest political issue. The first is that unlike wars, crime, terrorism or economic crises, it can't be blamed entirely on other people. All of us are responsible for it, and no one more so than those well-educated, cosmopolitan, well-traveled people who might be expected to care the most.

The second is that, while we know that its total global effects are disastrous, we are also aware that climate change, in most rich, temperate countries, has so far been kind to us. Never again – unless the Gulf Stream stops - will the United Kingdom suffer a freeze of the kind we experienced in 1947, 1963 or 1982. Never again need we worry that our summers will be rained off. Yes, we'd like a bit more rain in the summer for growing our vegetables, and a bit less rain in the winter, if we were stupid enough to have bought a house on the floodplain. But for most of us, most of the time, our pollution looks like a blessing. We caused this problem, but it's going to hurt us far less than some of the poorest people on the planet.

So we claim to worry about climate change, and we claim to wish that someone would do something. But in reality, we hope they don't. Otherwise we might have to change the way we live.

Looking at the crazy decisions people are still making, it seems to me that we are almost challenging the climate to prove us wrong. Cars are becoming bigger and flights more frequent. Just as the effects of climate change are becoming universally acknowledged, we have started buying air conditioners and patio heaters. The most celebrated architect on earth, Frank Gehry, now builds open-air auditoriums with *outdoor* air conditioning. It is beginning to look like the last days of the Roman empire.

So what the hell do we do about it? How do we turn the world's biggest problem into the world's biggest issue? I've been droning on about it for years and getting nowhere. The people who can be bothered to read my books and articles are, on the whole, the people who are interested already. Television could make climate change sexy, but it's controlled by people who see the death of the planet as a far less urgent problem than finding a parking place for their second Porsche.

In other words, we need a new Messiah. Or failing that, Kate Evans. She has brought something to this subject that none of the rest of us have managed: she has told the story of climate change in a way that's accessible, funny and moving. For a long time I've been telling her she's one of the best cartoonists alive today and she ought to pull her finger out and draw a daily strip for some august publication. But now I'm quite glad she hasn't, as she has spent her time producing something much more worthwhile. I loved her last book – *Copse* – and I love this one even more. If anyone can reach the people who don't give a damn about the biosphere, it's her – and you, if you buy this book and give it to someone who needs to read it.

CHAPTER 1

SO WHAT IS THIS GREENHOUSE EFFECT?

IN 1896, SWEDISH SCIENTIST SVANTE ARRHENIUS WORKED OUT HOW PUMPING **EXTRA CARBON DIOXIDE** INTO THE AIR, WITH THE LARGE-SCALE BURNING OF FOSSIL FUELS, IS **ADDING** TO THE NATURAL INSULATING PROPERTY OF THE ATMOSPHERE...

...IT'S NOW 2006 AND NO ONE SEEMS TO HAVE LISTENED VERY MUCH. HUMANS ARE DUMPING **7 BILLION TONS** OF CARBON DIOXIDE INTO THE ATMOSPHERE EACH YEAR. WE HAVE ARTIFICIALLY INCREASED THE AMOUNT OF CO_2 IN THE AIR BY A **THIRD**. ①

AT THE SAME TIME AS CO_2 (FROM FOSSIL FUEL BURNING) IS HOTTING THINGS UP, **SO_2**, THAT'S **SULFUR DIOXIDE** (ALSO FROM FOSSIL FUEL BURNING), FORMS SULFATE PARTICLES WHICH **COOL THE PLANET DOWN** BY REFLECTING INCOMING LIGHT BACK INTO SPACE. THESE TWO PROCESSES HAVE TO BE CONSIDERED TOGETHER TO GET AN ACCURATE PICTURE OF GLOBAL TEMPERATURE, BUT WHEN THEY ARE, IT'S CLEAR THAT **THINGS ARE GETTING WARMER**.

OTHER GASES CONTRIBUTE TO THE GREENHOUSE EFFECT. **METHANE** LEVELS HAVE RISEN 150%, **NITROUS OXIDE** HAS RISEN BY 15% AND MANMADE CHEMICALS **SULFUR HEXAFLUORIDE** AND **CFC**s HAVE BEEN FOUND TO HAVE A POWERFUL WARMING ACTION ON THE PLANET. ②

THE GREENHOUSE EFFECT ISN'T THE ONLY FACTOR THAT DETERMINES GLOBAL CLIMATE. **VOLCANIC ACTIVITY** AND **SUNSPOT CYCLES** ALSO PLAY A PART, BUT THESE NATURAL PHENOMENA **SHOULD** HAVE ACTED TO COOL THE PLANET DOWN OVER THE PAST 100 YEARS, NOT HEAT IT UP...

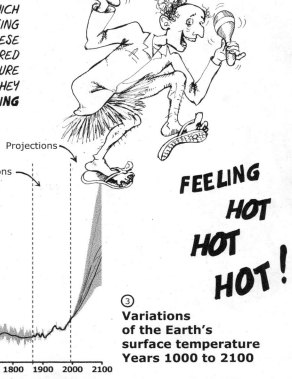

FEELING **HOT HOT HOT**!

Projections

Global instrumental observations

Observations (Northern Hemisphere proxy data)

③ **Variations of the Earth's surface temperature Years 1000 to 2100**

.0
.5
.0
.5
.0
.5
.0
.5
.0
.5
.0
.5
.0
.5

1000 1100 1200 1300 1400 1500 1600 1700 1800 1900 2000 2100

ASK YOURSELF, WILL **YOUR** GREENHOUSE BE AFFECTED?
THE ANSWER IS ALMOST CERTAINLY **YES**!

WHERE DO GREENHOUSE GASES COME FROM?

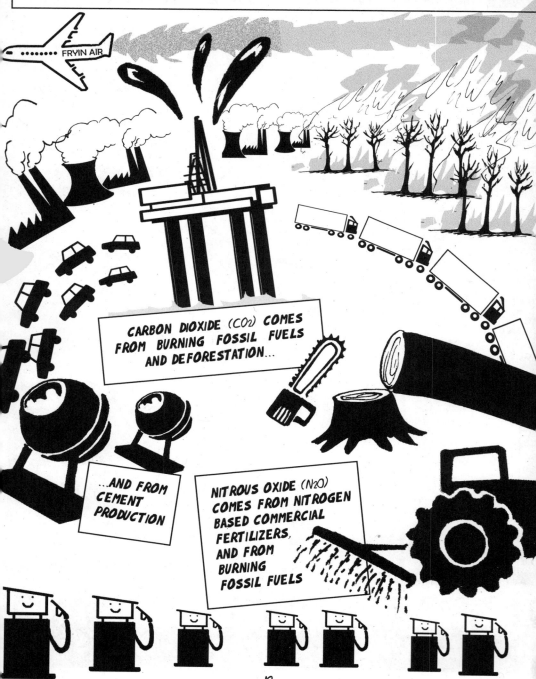

FRYIN AIR

CARBON DIOXIDE (CO2) COMES FROM BURNING FOSSIL FUELS AND DEFORESTATION...

...AND FROM CEMENT PRODUCTION

NITROUS OXIDE (N2O) COMES FROM NITROGEN BASED COMMERCIAL FERTILIZERS, AND FROM BURNING FOSSIL FUELS

METHANE COMES FROM FLOODING LAND FOR RICE PRODUCTION, AND FROM COW FARTS...

BBRRRP

METHANE LASTS FOR 12 YEARS IN THE ATMOSPHERE, NITROUS OXIDE LASTS FOR 120 YEARS, AND CO_2 FOR UP TO 200 YEARS.

...ALSO FROM LANDFILL SITES AND FROM LEAKS OF NATURAL GAS, WHILE CFCS ARE EMITTED BY VITAL, SOCIALLY NECESSARY, LIFE-ENRICHING SOFT DRINK DISPENSERS

DRINK Global warming

④

Hey, we can sort that. We could switch to renewable electricity production, introduce energy conservation measures, and cheap, efficient public transport, start running vehicles on biodiesel, build things with local materials, plant trees, go organic, eat curry and chips instead of rice and drink warm lemonade.

WHO SAYS CLIMATE CHANGE IS EVEN HAPPENING ANYWAY? I'M NOT CONVINCED! WE NEED MORE PROOF!!!

WHAT?!! ARE YOU SOME KIND OF DANGEROUS ENVIRONMENTAL EXTREMIST?!!!

13

WHO SAYS CLIMATE CHANGE IS REALLY HAPPENING?

CLIMATE CHANGE IS... ALREADY FULLY UNDERWAY

CLIMATE CHANGE IS REAL... PREPARE FOR THE CONSEQUENCES

Joint statement by the science academies of Brazil, Canada, China, France, Germany, India, Italy, Japan, Russia, the UK and the US

Thomas Loster, chief executive of insurance corporation Munich Re Foundation

CLIMATE CHANGE IS A WEAPON OF MASS DESTRUCTION

Sir John Houghton, co-chair of the UN Intergovernmental Panel on Climate Change

George Carey, former Archbishop of Canterbury

OUR ENERGY-BURNING LIFESTYLES ARE PUSHING OUR PLANET TO THE POINT OF NO RETURN.

CLIMATE CHANGE IS THE MOST SEVERE PROBLEM THAT WE ARE FACING TODAY — MORE SERIOUS EVEN THAN THE THREAT OF TERRORISM

THE EVIDENCE IS THERE. THE DAMAGE IS BEING DONE.

Sir David King, chief scientific adviser to the UK government

Margaret Thatcher, British prime minister, speaking in 1989

[mumble mumble] ...major long term problem... [mumble]

LA LA LA LA
I'm not listening!

George W. Bush, US president

15

PROOF?

IN 1988, THE UNITED NATIONS SET UP THE **INTERGOVERNMENTAL PANEL ON CLIMATE CHANGE** (IPCC); AN INTERNATIONAL TEAM OF 2000 TOP SCIENTISTS AND **CLIMATE MODELERS** WHO TRACK AND PREDICT TRENDS IN CLIMATE CHANGE.

Let's just put a bit of desert in here.

HOT WIND

SAND

GLUE

Amazon

PLAY DOUGH

BALSA WOOD

COLD WIND

rica

IN 2001, THEY DECIDED THAT GLOBAL WARMING IS

attributable to human activities. ⑤

THE WORLD IS NOW 0.8°C WARMER THAN IN PRE-INDUSTRIAL TIMES. ⑥

0.8°C? THAT'S NOTHING! TINY! TINY! TINY!!!

Well, it isn't much, but since most of the planet is covered in deep water it takes a long time to heat up. At least 40 years. ⑦

So what we're seeing now is the effect of CO_2 emissions in the 1960s.

TOP SCIENTISTS THINK

Raising the temperature of the world by just 1°C means pumping an incredible extra amount of energy into the weather system. Recent studies say we could be in line for a 10°C rise and during the last **ICE AGE** the planet was only 5°C colder than today.

www.climate prediction.net ⑧

Oh

What are you reading?

That's not on the National Curriculum.

It's just getting a bit warmer, that's all.

Everyone likes a bit of sunshine, don't they?

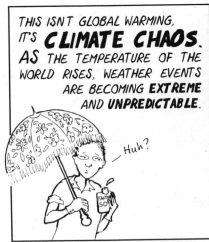

THIS ISN'T GLOBAL WARMING, IT'S **CLIMATE CHAOS**. AS THE TEMPERATURE OF THE WORLD RISES, WEATHER EVENTS ARE BECOMING **EXTREME** AND **UNPREDICTABLE**.

— Huh?

FACTOR 50

WIND IS CAUSED BY THE DIFFERENCE BETWEEN ATMOSPHERIC HIGH AND LOW PRESSURE. WITH MORE ENERGY (FROM HEAT) BUZZING AROUND IN THE SYSTEM, THE HIGHS GET HIGHER, THE LOWS GET LOWER AND THE WINDS GET STRONGER.

IT'S GETTING A BIT **WINDIER** AND **STORMIER**.

HEAT SOAKS INTO THE SEA AND BOUNCES OFF LAND. THIS MAKES THE AIR ABOVE THE SEA COOLER THAN ABOVE LAND. MORE HEAT MAKES FOR A BIGGER TEMPERATURE DIFFERENCE, AND STRONG WINDS + CYCLONES RESULT.

Hmm — that looks completely pear-shaped.

COOLER AIR   WARMER AIR

What about "Xylophone"?

No, it has to be a girl's name.

Isn't that a girl's name?

IN 2005, THERE WERE SO MANY TROPICAL STORMS OVER THE ATLANTIC THAT FOR THE FIRST TIME EVER, FORECASTERS RAN OUT OF NAMES FOR THEM.

We're not in Kansas now, Toto.

⑨ CLIMATE CHANGE HAS INCREASED THE DESTRUCTIVE POWER OF HURRICANES BY 70%

We tried to leave but the roads were jammed. We did a third of a mile in an hour.

This is even more dangerous. We'd be safer in our house.

So we went back home.

Around 4 a.m. the wind picked up...

Bloop Bloop

The house was shaking in the wind, blowing like a freight train.

What the?

Mom?

Zahria, run get some towels, Junior, wake up.

The towels were useless. Outside the glass was two feet of waves.

CRASH

What was that

Hush

Those are my toys in the water

This is comin up way too fast

By now the only way out of the house was to swim.

Our street was a river.

I didn't know cars floated.

Our lives were in the air.

IT'S GETTING A BIT **WETTER**.

"GLOBAL WARMING" ISN'T ALL ABOUT SUNSHINE. NOW WHEN IT RAINS, IT RAINS HARDER. THIS IS BECAUSE WARMER AIR CAN HOLD MORE WATER VAPOR BEFORE IT DROPS IT ALL AS RAIN, OR SNOW, OR HAIL.

Ah, me. An English Summer. All this rain will be good for the garden.

THESE DAYS, THE UK GETS **TWICE AS MANY HEAVY DOWNPOURS** OF RAIN AS IT DID IN THE 1960S. ⑪

THAT'S THE KIND OF RAIN THAT FLATTENS CROPS, OVERWHELMS SEWERS, CAUSES DRIVERS TO CRASH THEIR CARS, AND RIVERS TO BURST THEIR BANKS.

CO_2 H_2O

HERE'S ANOTHER THING: PLANTS "BREATHE" CO_2, AND WITH MORE OF IT IN THE AIR, THEY NEED TO BREATHE LESS. SO LESS WATER VAPOR EVAPORATES FROM THEIR LEAVES, AND MORE GETS LEFT IN THE SOIL. ⑫

SATURATED SOIL + HEAVY RAIN? THAT = **FLOODS!**

20

Just hang on a minute. These are natural weather events. You can't say they're caused by climate change.

But the scientists agree that global warming will cause severe storms and floods.

Yes.

And now we're getting severe storms and floods.

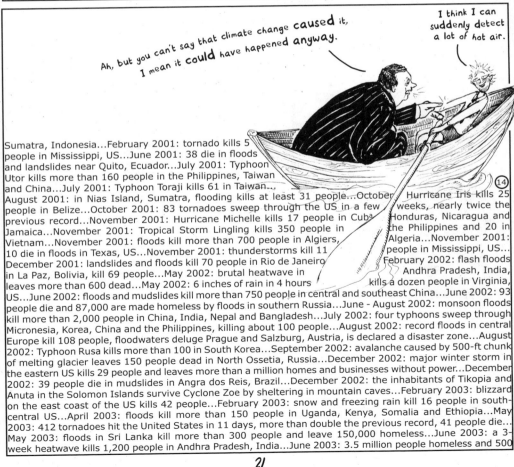

Decem...ber 1999...enezuela, flooding and mudslides kill up to 20,000 people...February 2000: flooding in Mozambia...and Zimbabwe kills 700 and leaves 280,000 homeless...July 2000:heatwave in Italy and the Balkans kills dozens and damages crops...August 2000: Typhoon Bilis kills 11 people in Taiwan...September 2000: rising floodwaters from the Mekong River kill 235 in Vietnam, Cambodia and Thailand, and leave 4.5 million people homeless...November 2000: 7.2 million acres of the western US burn in forest fires...November 2000: 119 people die in floods in

Ah, but you can't say that climate change caused it, I mean it could have happened anyway.

I think I can suddenly detect a lot of hot air.

Sumatra, Indonesia...February 2001: tornado kills 5 people in Mississippi, US...June 2001: 38 die in floods and landslides near Quito, Ecuador...July 2001: Typhoon Utor kills more than 160 people in the Philippines, Taiwan and China...July 2001: Typhoon Toraji kills 61 in Taiwan...August 2001: in Nias Island, Sumatra, flooding kills at least 31 people...October Hurricane Iris kills 25 people in Belize...October 2001: 83 tornadoes sweep through the US in a few weeks, nearly twice the previous record...November 2001: Hurricane Michelle kills 17 people in Cuba, Honduras, Nicaragua and Jamaica...November 2001: Tropical Storm Lingling kills 350 people in the Philippines and 20 in Vietnam...November 2001: floods kill more than 700 people in Algiers, Algeria...November 2001: 10 die in floods in Texas, US...November 2001: thunderstorms kill 11 people in Mississippi, US...December 2001: landslides and floods kill 70 people in Rio de Janeiro February 2002: flash floods in La Paz, Bolivia, kill 69 people...May 2002: brutal heatwave in Andhra Pradesh, India, leaves more than 600 dead...May 2002: 6 inches of rain in 4 hours kills a dozen people in Virginia, US...June 2002: floods and mudslides kill more than 750 people in central and southeast China...June 2002: 93 people die and 87,000 are made homeless by floods in southern Russia...June - August 2002: monsoon floods kill more than 2,000 people in China, India, Nepal and Bangladesh...July 2002: four typhoons sweep through Micronesia, Korea, China and the Philippines, killing about 100 people...August 2002: record floods in central Europe kill 108 people, floodwaters deluge Prague and Salzburg, Austria, is declared a disaster zone...August 2002: Typhoon Rusa kills more than 100 in South Korea...September 2002: avalanche caused by 500-ft chunk of melting glacier leaves 150 people dead in North Ossetia, Russia...December 2002: major winter storm in the eastern US kills 29 people and leaves more than a million homes and businesses without power...December 2002: 39 people die in mudslides in Angra dos Reis, Brazil...December 2002: the inhabitants of Tikopia and Anuta in the Solomon Islands survive Cyclone Zoe by sheltering in mountain caves...February 2003: blizzard on the east coast of the US kills 42 people...February 2003: snow and freezing rain kill 16 people in south-central US...April 2003: floods kill more than 150 people in Uganda, Kenya, Somalia and Ethiopia...May 2003: 412 tornadoes hit the United States in 11 days, more than double the previous record, 41 people die... May 2003: floods in Sri Lanka kill more than 300 people and leave 150,000 homeless...June 2003: a 3-week heatwave kills 1,200 people in Andhra Pradesh, India...June 2003: 3.5 million people homeless and 500

⑭

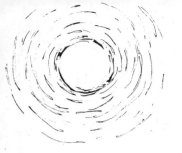

IT'S GETTING A BIT **HOTTER** (OF COURSE)

THIS BOOK WAS WRITTEN IN 2006. **2005 WAS THE HOTTEST YEAR** ON RECORD. **EIGHT** OUT OF THE PAST **TEN** YEARS HAVE TOPPED THE TEMPERATURE CHARTS.[13]

We prepared our fields for planting seeds in the November rains. We waited but the first drop didn't fall until December 20th. After a day, the rains stopped.

30% OF THE WORLD IS NOW AFFECTED BY DROUGHT. [16] THAT'S MORE THAN **TWICE** AS MUCH AS IN THE 1970S.

IT'S SIMPLE. **MORE WATER EVAPORATES FROM HOT SOIL.** EVENTUALLY IT DOES FALL BACK TO EARTH AS RAIN, BUT THE NEW CRAZY WIND PATTERNS MEAN THAT **IT'S NOW FALLING IN THE WRONG PLACE, AT THE WRONG TIME.**

IN 2005, THE UN WARNED THAT **ONE IN SIX COUNTRIES** WAS EXPERIENCING **DROUGHT-RELATED FOOD SHORTAGES,** AND THAT THIS IS PART OF **A NEW LONG-TERM TREND.** [17]

I had 100 goats and sold ten of them.
The others all died.

WHEN TEMPERATURES HIT **50°C** IN INDIA IN 2005, HEAT STRESS KILLED 1,500 PEOPLE.

PHEW WHAT A SCORCHER

Oh no. A watering ban.

AND IN THE EUROPEAN HEATWAVE OF JULY 2003, 39,000 ELDERLY AND VULNERABLE PEOPLE DIED.[18]

FOREST FIRES SPREAD FURTHER AND FASTER IN HOT, DRY CONDITIONS: IN 1997-8 **TEN MILLION HECTARES** OF INDONESIAN RAINFOREST BURNED, RELEASING AS MUCH CO_2 AS EUROPE DOES IN A YEAR.[19]

70% OF **AFRICANS** RELY ON RAIN-FED AGRICULTURE TO SURVIVE, IN A CONTINENT WHERE FERTILE LANDS ARE RAPIDLY TURNING TO **DESERT**.

NOW, IN 2006, **17 MILLION** PEOPLE ARE CURRENTLY **STARVING** IN **MALAWI**, **NIGER**, **SOMALIA**, **ETHIOPIA** AND **KENYA**. [20]

AND IN THE NEXT 35 YEARS, WATER SUPPLIES IN SOUTHERN AFRICA ARE PREDICTED TO **FALL BY HALF**. [21]

100 MILLION PEOPLE WILL BE AFFECTED.

"terrible natural disaster here in Kenya"

Green Beans produce of Kenya

Kenya?

Hey, kids. Show you care. Buy a wristband and download this feel-good single.

Omigod! It's Barb Gandalf!

♩ ♪ 🎵 **THERE MIGHT NOT BE SNOW IN AFRICA THIS CHRISTMASTIME** 🎵

Hey, this is plastic. It's made of fossil fuels.

Gosh, indeed, no snow. Did you know that the snow has melted at the summit of Mount Kilimanjaro for the first time in 11,000 years... [22]

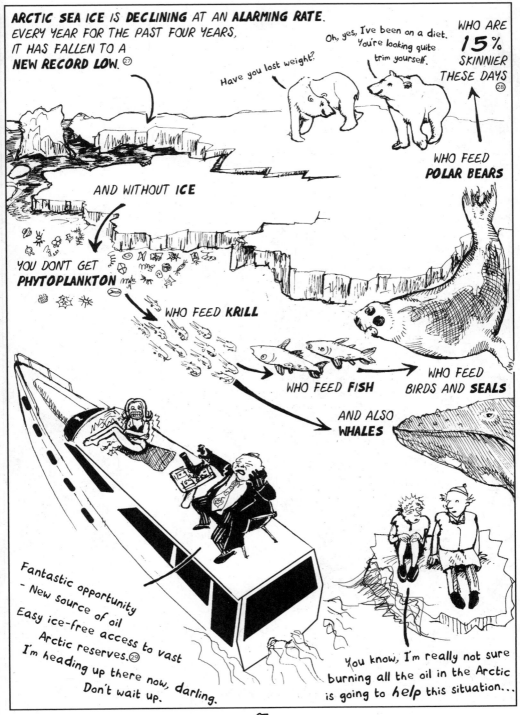

SEA ICE MELTING IS OK. WHEN ICE CUBES MELT IN A DRINK, THE DRINK DOESN'T OVERFLOW. IT'S WHEN ICE ON THE LAND MELTS INTO THE SEA THAT THE VOLUME OF WATER INCREASES.

BUT ANTARCTICA AND GREENLAND ARE COVERED WITH HUGE LAND-BASED ICE SHEETS.

WELL, THE ARCTIC IS MAINLY SEA ICE, SO THAT'S OK

REMEMBER HOW WARMING IS HAPPENING FASTEST AT THE POLES?

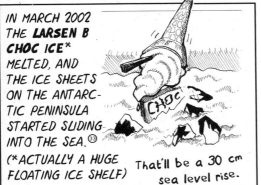

IN MARCH 2002 THE LARSEN B CHOC ICE* MELTED, AND THE ICE SHEETS ON THE ANTARCTIC PENINSULA STARTED SLIDING INTO THE SEA. [33] (*ACTUALLY A HUGE FLOATING ICE SHELF)

That'll be a 30 cm sea level rise.

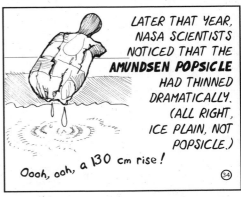

LATER THAT YEAR, NASA SCIENTISTS NOTICED THAT THE AMUNDSEN POPSICLE HAD THINNED DRAMATICALLY. (ALL RIGHT, ICE PLAIN, NOT POPSICLE.)

Oooh, ooh, a 130 cm rise! [34]

IN 2004, GREENLAND'S GLACIERS STARTED MELTING TWICE AS FAST. [35]

Look, a 3°C rise triggers runaway melting...

...and then what happens when the West Antarctic Ice Sheet breaks off the little islands it's sitting on and floats away?

SPLOSH

I give up. What happens then?

Gosh, one 7 meter sea level rise and another 7 meter sea level rise makes, um, have you got a calculator? [36]

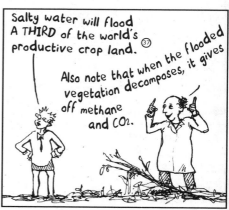

ADD THIS UP, AND IT MAKES FOR A HUGELY UNSTABLE GLOBAL POLITICAL OUTLOOK. **WARS** WILL BE FOUGHT, FOR WATER AND FOR LAND.[39]

Hmm, drought. Now this country overextracts water for irrigation from its major rivers. Ah, the neighbor downstream invades! They want to settle the surplus population uprooted by flooding on the coast. Oh great, a double six
– major cyclones hit the area. Can you pass me the hairdryer?

NEEEOW

BRRRR

LAND MINES

GUIDANCE SYSTEMS

GEC Shares Certificate

ARMS SALES

LOCKHEED MARTIN WEAPONS COMPONENTS FOR EXPORT

Shame.

CLIMATE CHAOS HAS ALREADY FORCED 25 MILLION PEOPLE TO LEAVE THEIR HOMES.[40] WE CAN EXPECT TO SEE 200 MILLION MORE CLIMATE REFUGEES BY THE MIDDLE OF THE CENTURY.

REFUGEES?!!

THEY'RE NOT COMING HERE !!!

AND THERE'S **MORE!** WHAT ABOUT THE EFFECTS ON **WILDLIFE?** AS OUR ECOSYSTEMS FACE *MELTDOWN*

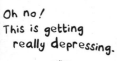

Oh no! This is getting really depressing.

MOST SPECIES ON EARTH ARE ADAPTED TO A PARTICULAR SET OF CLIMATIC CONDITIONS. NOW THAT THE TEMPERATURE IS RISING, **THEY HAVE TO MOVE** TO STAY COOL.

This isn't going to be easy.

HABITAT LOSS IS SO SEVERE, **WHERE ARE THEY GOING TO MOVE TO?**

SLOW **PLANTS** CAN MOVE AT 0.04 KM A YEAR

WHILE REALLY SPEEDY ONES CAN SPREAD THEIR SEEDS 2 KM A YEAR.

TO KEEP PACE WITH CLIMATE CHANGE PLANTS NEED TO BE ABLE TO MOVE 1.5 TO 5.5 KM A YEAR.[41] **MOST PLANTS CAN'T MOVE FAST ENOUGH.**

Peter! Heidi!

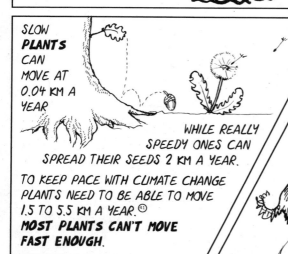

Wow, even these remote Siberian lakes are showing dramatic ecological changes. Can't blame that on local pollution.[42]

IT'S NOT GOOD NEWS FOR **ALPINE ECOSYSTEMS**. SPECIALIZED SPECIES ARE RETREATING UP THE SLOPES INTO **AN EVER-DECREASING AREA OF LAND.**

CORAL REEFS CAN'T MOVE, AND THEY ARE INCREDIBLY TEMPERATURE SENSITIVE. IF THE SEA WARMS BY JUST 2° C, MOST FORMS OF CORAL **BLEACH** AND DIE.

A QUARTER OF ALL SPECIES OF FISH LIVE ON CORAL REEFS. CLIMATE CHAOS HAS KILLED 92% OF REEFS IN THE WESTERN INDIAN OCEAN [43]

SAND EELS HAVE HAD NO PROBLEM MOVING INTO COOLER WATERS AWAY FROM THE NORTH COAST OF SCOTLAND...

BUT NOW THE **PUFFINS** THAT BREED THERE HAVE BEEN LEFT WITH NO FOOD FOR THEIR CHICKS. ANOTHER LINK IN THE FOOD CHAIN HAS COME UNDONE.

THE WAY THINGS ARE GOING, IN **OUR** LIFETIMES WE'RE GOING **TO SEE** BETWEEN A **THIRD** AND A **HALF** OF ALL LAND **ANIMALS** AND **PLANTS** BECOME **EXTINCT** [45]

PARTICULARLY AT RISK ARE ANIMALS HIGH UP THE FOOD CHAIN, SUCH AS **WHALES**, **POLAR BEARS**, **GRIZZLY BEARS**, **TIGERS** AND **GIANT PANDAS**.

But ("sniff") those are all the cute ones! Look - I've got pandas on my pencil case. Pandas can't die out. ("sniff sniff")

Well, you win some you lose some.

TRUE, SOME SPECIES STAND TO GAIN FROM CLIMATE CHANGE.

ARMIES WERE MOBILIZED TO FIGHT **LOCUST** SWARMS THAT DEVASTATED CROPS IN **WEST AFRICA** IN SEPTEMBER 2004.

TENSHUN! FIX FLY SWATTERS READY, AIM... SWAT TEAM - KILL!

CLUNK

RECORD NUMBERS DESCENDED ON **FRANCE** IN JULY 2005. [46]

What's for dinner?

Spruce bark again.

Yum yum

My favorite.

THE **SPRUCE BARK BEETLE** IS THRIVING. [47] IT'S MUNCHED UP 2.3 MILLION ALASKAN SPRUCE TREES SINCE 1992.

IT'S LOOKING GOOD FOR **RATS** AS THEIR NATURAL PREDATORS DIE OUT..

I'll just turn up the patio heater.

Global warming? Bring it on! I had these cigars air-freighted in from Havana.

COCKROACHES HAVE BEEN WITH US FOR MILLENNIA. THEY'LL BE JUST FINE.

34

MOST WORRYINGLY, IT'S BOOM TIME FOR THE **ANOPHELES MOSQUITO**, THE MOST DANGEROUS ANIMAL IN THE WORLD...

AS IT GETS **WARMER**, THIS **MALARIA-CARRYING** PEST FLIES TO **HIGHER ALTITUDES**, IT **INCREASES ITS RANGE** (TO PLACES LIKE EUROPE AND NORTH AMERICA), IT **BREEDS MORE RAPIDLY** AND **BITES MORE OFTEN**, AND THE PARASITE IN ITS GUT MULTIPLIES MORE QUICKLY, **DOUBLING** THE CHANCE OF **DISEASE TRANSMISSION**. [48]

MALARIA **CURRENTLY KILLS ONE CHILD EVERY 30 SECONDS**, AND IT AFFECTS [49] 45% OF THE WORLD'S POPULATION. WHAT WILL IT BE LIKE WHEN THIS SPREADS TO 60%?

AND DON'T FORGET THE **AEDES AEGYPTI MOSQUITO**, WHICH SPREADS **DENGUE FEVER** AND **YELLOW FEVER**.

MOSQUITOES BREED IN **STAGNANT POOLS OF WATER**, JUST LIKE THOSE THAT ARE LEFT BEHIND AFTER **MAJOR FLOODS**.

IN SEPTEMBER 1999 IN **NEW YORK**, [50] **HELICOPTERS** SPRAYED PESTICIDE OVER THE CITY TO HALT THE SPREAD OF A NEW, MOSQUITO-BORNE DISEASE...

...IT WAS **WEST NILE VIRUS**, NOT MALARIA, THIS TIME.

VIRUSES, BACTERIA AND **PARASITES** BREED MORE READILY IN THE NEW WARMER CONDITIONS... [51]

Ooh. Look at this.

OH MY GOD! WE'RE ALL GOING TO DIE!!!

Tsk tsk. These adolescent mood swings.

Don't worry your pretty little head about it. These things only affect people in HOT countries. And those people tend to die a lot anyway.

Ooh more interest payments on those loans. Marvelous.

Here in England it will be balmy... ...Mediterranean...

Um, no.

OUR MILD CLIMATE IS DUE TO THE **GULF STREAM** WHICH BRINGS WARM, TROPICAL WATER OVER FROM THE CARIBBEAN. THE GULF STREAM COULD **SHUT DOWN**.

It doesn't feel very tropical to me.

Look, here and here in the North Atlantic, these cold patches drive the ocean currents.

NORTH POLE

GREEN-LAND

COLD

COLD

DEEP

SALTY HOT WATER

COLD WATER

NORTH AMERICA

EUROPE

AFRICA

SOUTH AMERICA

HOT WATER

WHAT HAPPENS IS, THE **SUN** SHINING ON THE CARIBBEAN **EVAPORATES** OFF SOME WATER AND MAKES THE SEA **EXTRA SALTY**. THIS HOT SALTY WATER FLOATS MERRILY ACROSS THE ATLANTIC, **DUMPING HEAT** ON EUROPE IN THE PROCESS. **THAT'S THE GULF STREAM**.

WHEN IT GETS UP NEXT TO **GREENLAND**, SUDDENLY, IT'S **VERY COLD**, AND THE WATER, BEING EXTRA SALTY, IS EXTRA **DENSE**. IT **SINKS TO THE OCEAN FLOOR**. NOW IT'S PART OF THE **NORTH ATLANTIC DEEP WATER**, A VERY **DEEP**, **SALTY**, VERY **SLOW** CURRENT. IT'LL TAKE A **THOUSAND YEARS** TO LIGHTEN UP AND COME ROUND AGAIN.

EUROPE GETS A **MILLION POWER STATIONS'** WORTH OF HEAT FROM THE GULF STREAM

ALL YOU NEED TO DO TO HALT THIS MIGHTY OCEAN FLOW IS TO **ADD** MORE **FRESH, UNSALTY WATER** TO THAT SALTY WATER IN THE NORTH ATLANTIC. SAY, BY **MELTING** SOME **GLACIERS** IN CANADA AND GREENLAND... IT'S HAPPENED BEFORE, AND IT COULD BE HAPPENING AGAIN. **IT LOOKS LIKE THE GULF STREAM HAS SLOWED BY 30% SINCE 1992!** [52]

IF THE GULF STREAM **STOPS** ALTOGETHER, IT **WILL** AFFECT WEATHER PATTERNS AROUND THE WORLD. [53]

This is mayhem! Crops fail in India! Sea levels rise in the North Atlantic! The Amazon rainforest dies out! Europe gets a mini Ice Age!

ICE

And England ends up 10°C **colder** in winter. Look, We're way further north than Montreal.

MONTREAL
X

LONDON

Gosh, in that case I'll have to consider relocating abroad.

But that'll make you a refugee.

Oh no no no no no.

It makes me an expatriate.

1) Special Report on Climate Change, www.guardianunlimited.co.uk.

2) Simon Retallack and Peter Bunyard, "We're Changing Our Climate! Who Can Doubt It?" *The Ecologist*, March-April, 1999.

3) Intergovernmental Panel on Climate Change (IPCC) Third Assessment Report, *Climate Change 2001, Summary for Policymakers*. This graph is popularly known as the hockey-stick graph; for an interesting investigation of the science behind it, see "Climate: The Great Hockey Stick Debate," *New Scientist*, March 18, 2006.

4) Sources and rates of decomposition of greenhouse gases from Guy Dauncey, *Stormy Weather: 101 Solutions to Global Climate Change* and from *The Ecologist*, March-April, 1999.

5) IPCC Third Assessment Report, *Summary for Policymakers*.

6) Temperature rise from the late 19th century to 2003 from the Hadley Centre for Climate Prediction and Research, *Uncertainty, Risk and Dangerous Climate Change: Recent Research on Climate Change*, December 2004, www.metoffice.com/research/hadleycentre.

7) This phenomenon is referred to as the "thermal inertia" of the planet. Research by Tom Wigley at NCAR and Gerald Meehl, National Center for Atmospheric Research, *New Scientist*, March 17, 2005 and from *The Ecologist*, March-April, 1999.

8) A rise of 10°C is among the scenarios predicted by www.climateprediction.net, a distributed-computing project by Oxford University. The range of predicted scenarios ran from 1.9°C to 11.5°C. "There is no evidence that temperatures have ever been as high as in some of the climateprediction.net simulations." *New Scientist*, January 26, 2005. See also Meinrat Andreae, Max Planck Institute for Chemistry, and Peter Cox and Chris Jones, Hadley Centre, who predict a temperature rise of 6°C to 10°C. "Clearing Smoke May Trigger Global Warming Rise," *New Scientist*, June 29, 2005.

9) Kerry Emanuel, Massachusetts Institute of Technology, *Nature*, Vol. 436, 686 (*New Scientist*, December 12, 2005). P. Webster and J. Curry, Georgia Institute of Technology, concluded in September 2005 that the number of intense hurricanes around the world has almost doubled in the past 35 years (*New Scientist*, March 16, 2006).

10) "In September, Sir John Houghton, chair of the Royal Commission on Environmental Pollution, said unequivocally that the superpowerful hurricanes battering the United States were the 'smoking gun' of global warming." *The Independent*, January 5, 2006. All text gleaned from Hurricane Katrina eyewitness testimony, principally "zeta psi" at www.unsolvedmysteries.com with additional words from www.survivedkatrina.org; "One Girl's Escape Story from Hurricane Katrina," CBBC Newsround; "Policing the Venice from Hell" and We Knew It Was Going to Happen," BBC.co.uk;

and Jim Edds, www.extremestorms.co.uk.

11) P. Frich et al, "Observed Coherent Changes in Climate Extremes During the Second Half of the 20th Century," *Climate Research*, Vol. 19, No. 3, 193-212, 2002 and T. Osborn et al, "Observed Trends in the Daily Intensity of United Kingdom Precipitation," *International Journal of Climatology*, March 24, 2000, Vol. 20, 347-364. Both quoted in Mark Lynas, *High Tide: The Truth About Our Climate Crisis*.

12) Richard Betts, Hadley Centre, has calculated that the reduced uptake of groundwater by plants could increase groundwater by 10% over the next century. "Climatologists Give Waterworld Warning for Earth," *New Scientist*, April 26, 2003.

13) Christian Aid. *Unnatural Disasters: Climate Change and Developing Countries*, May 2000.

14) Statistics from www.infoplease.com.

15) NASA's Goddard Institute for Space Studies concluded that 2005 was the hottest year on record. The UK Meteorological Office and the US National Oceanic and Atmospheric Administration disagreed and found that 1998 was marginally warmer. The temperature rise in 1998 was partly due to the El Niño phenomenon (a natural wobble in climatic conditions) while the 2005 high temperatures cannot be attributed to such an event. "2005 Continues the Warming Trend," *Washington Post*, December 16, 2005.

16) Research by Kevin Trenberth et al at the National Center for Atmospheric Research, Boulder, Colorado. Their statement to the American Meteorological Society was reported in *New Scientist*, January 22, 2005. The research found very little difference in global drought conditions between 1870 and 1970, and a marked increase from 1970 on.

17) John Vidal and Tim Radford, "Climate Change: One in Six Countries Facing Food Shortage," *The Guardian*, June 30, 2005. The words that accompany the illustrations of African famine on pp. 25 and 26 are those of African farmers and nomadic herders, respectively. From John Vidal, "In the Land Where Life Is on Hold," *The Guardian*, June 30, 2005, and Jeevan Vasagar, "Meagre Food for Babies First and Elderly Last, as Villages Empty of Life," *The Guardian*, August 4, 2005.

18) Christian Aid, *The Climate of Poverty: Facts, Fears and Hope*, May 2006, 8.

19) Kevin Tohurst, senior lecturer in fire ecology and management, University of Melbourne, has warned that climate change will bring "an increased number of larger, more devastating wildfires." University of Melbourne press release, December 9, 2003. Ten million hectares statistic is from Dinyar Godrej, *The No-Nonsense Guide to Climate Change*.

20) This figure is totaled from Wikipedia reports of drought-related food crises in Niger, Malawi and the Horn of Africa.

21) A 10% drop in rainfall translates into a 50%

drop in available surface water due to increased aridity at higher temperatures, as calculated by Maarten de Wit, University of Cape Town. *New Scientist*, March 11, 2006.

22) Georg Kaser, University of Innsbruck, states that "there is a strong link between conditions on Kilimanjaro and global warming" in the face of some scientific debate on the subject. Fred Pearce, "Global Warming: The Flaw in the Thaw," *New Scientist*, August 27, 2005. Richard Taylor, Department of Geography, University College of London, published a study in *Geophysical Research Letters* (May 17, 2006) in which it is estimated that all the equatorial ice caps of the Rwenzori Mountains of East Africa will disappear in the next 20 years.

23) *Uggianaqtuq* is a Baffin Island Inuit word for unexpected and unpredictable. They get to use it a lot when talking about the weather these days.

24) P. Prestrud, "Arctic Climate Impact Assessment Report," *New Scientist*, November 2, 2004.

25) Based on an account by Mark Lynas in *High Tide*. I nicked the joke about Baked Alaska from him, too. There aren't that many laughs to be had about climate change.

26) Caribou starvation due to icing of lichen on tundra from the 2004 Arctic Climate Assessment Report, quoted in Tim Flannery, *The Weather Makers*, 100.

27) Statement by the US National Snow and Ice Data Center, University of Colorado. *New Scientist*, September 29, 2005.

28) Tim Appenzeller et al, "The Heat Is On," *National Geographic*, September 2004, quoted in *The Weather Makers*, 102.

29) P. Prestrud, researcher for the 2004 Arctic Climate Impact Assessment Report stated that about 25% of the earth's remaining oil reserves are in the Arctic, and that "for the oil industry, it will be an advantage if the ice disappears, increasing access to oil and gas reserves." *New Scientist*, November 2, 2005.

30) George Monbiot, *The Guardian*, August 10, 2004. See also Geoffrey Lean, "Ice-capped roof of world turns to desert," *The Independent*, May 7, 2006.

31) See James Bruges *The Little Earth Book* for a critique of the World Bank and IMF and an explanation of Third World vs First World debts and obligations.

32) *The Ecologist*, March/April, 1999.

33) "If the ice on the [Antarctic] peninsula melts entirely it will raise global sea levels by 0.3 metres, and the West Antarctic Ice Sheet contains enough water to contribute metres more." J. Hogan, "Antarctic Ice Sheet Is an 'Awakened Giant,'" *New Scientist*, February 2, 2005.

34) P. Thomas et al, "Accelerated Sea-level Rise from West Antarctica," *Science*, September 23, 2004, reported in *The Weather Makers*, 148: "As there is enough ice in the glaciers feeding into the Amundsen Sea to raise global sea levels by 1.3 metres, their increasing rate of flow, and the incipient break-up of their ice-plain 'brake,' are of concern to everyone."

35) Jonathan Gregory, University of Reading, and glaciologist Philippe Huybrechts, Free University, Brussels, have concluded that a 3°C temperature rise will provide a trigger for runaway melting, *New Scientist*, April 7, 2004. See also research by Adrian Luckman, University of Wales, which suggests a "sudden and synchronous" acceleration in the melting of Greenland's glaciers, *New Scientist*, February 11, 2006.

36) *The Weather Makers*, 149. In addition, Jim Hansen, director of NASA's Goddard Institute for Space Studies, has stated that the collapse of the Greenland ice sheet could be "explosively rapid," with sea levels rising "a couple of metres this century, and several more next century." *New Scientist*, February 4, 2006. See also report of the findings of glaciologists at the Royal Society, London. "Antarctic Ice Slipping Faster into the Sea," *New Scientist*, October 22, 2005.

37) *The Ecologist*, March/April 1999.

38) *High Tide*, 114. Also contains an amazing account of life on Tuvalu.

39) See Michael T. Klare, *Resource Wars: The New Landscape of Global Conflict* (Owl, 2001).

40) Calculation on environmental refugees by Norman Myers, reported by George Monbiot, *The Guardian*, July 29, 1999. The Red Cross uses the same estimate for the current number of environmental refugees in World Disaster Reports 2002. See also a statement by the United Nations University's Institute for Environment and Human Security (May 3, 2006) which estimates the number of environmental refugees will reach 50 million by 2010 and calls for the international community to define, recognize and extend support to this new category of refugee (www.oneworld.net).

41) *The No-Nonsense Guide to Climate Change*, 81-82.

42) J. Smol, Queen's University, Kingston, Ontario, researched sediment cores from 45 remote Arctic lakes and found evidence of "regime shifts" in their ecologies that are synchronous with rising temperature. *New Scientist*, March 5, 2005.

43) N. Graham, University of Newcastle Upon Tyne, surveyed the health of coral reefs in the Seychelles north of Madagascar and found that coral cover was at 7.5% of pre-1998 levels. Proceedings of the National Academy of Sciences, May 16, 2006. In a report on the study, Nancy Knowlton, a marine biology professor at Scripps Institution of Oceanography, La Jolla, California, says, "by and large, reefs have collapsed catastrophically just in the three decades that I've been studying them." *National Geographic News*, May 16, 2005.

44) 2004 and 2005 saw record low numbers of breeding sea birds in the north of Scotland. Marine warden Sarah Money commented, "This is a really worrying sign that something is badly wrong with

the health of our seas." *The Telegraph*, July 28, 2005. For a description of the extent of the collapse, see "Seabirds in the North Sea: Victims of Climate Change?" *Birdlife International*, May 1, 2005.

45) C. Thomas et al, University of Leeds, January 2004. Projected extinctions by 2050 under the IPCC's "business as usual" scenario. Even with drastic, immediate cuts in CO2, an estimated 9% of land species face extinction. *New Scientist*, January 7, 2004.

46) "Africa Declares 'War' on Locusts," bbc.co.uk, September 1, 2004, and "Plague of Locusts Invades France," *The Observer*, July 17, 2005.

47) *High Tide*, 60.

48) *The No-Nonsense Guide to Climate Change*, 46-47, which also states that the altitude at which the Anopheles mosquito breeds has increased by 500 feet in 30 years. This has led to new outbreaks of disease in Kenya, Ethiopia, Rwanda, Tanzania, Uganda, Zimbabwe, Papua New Guinea and West Papua.

49) Médecins sans Frontières, "Effective Medical Care in Crisis Situations," April 2006.

50) *The No-Nonsense Guide to Climate Change*, 46. The disease recurred in 2000.

51) Christian Aid, *The Climate of Poverty: Facts, Fears and Hope*, May 2006, 11. By the end of the century, 182 million people in Sub-Saharan Africa could die of diseases directly attributed to climate change. In addition to mosquito-borne disease, diarrhea, cholera, Rift Valley fever, leishmaniasis and meningitis are predicted to increase.

52) Harry Bryden, National Oceanography Centre, Southampton. *The Independent*, November 30, 2005. Bryden's team found that the flow remained steady between 1957 and 1992, then tailed off dramatically. Commenting on the findings, Tore Furevik, University of Bergen, said, "There are certainly large changes going on beneath the surface of the North Atlantic, but we are still missing too many pieces of the puzzle to know what they are." *New Scientist*, April 15, 2006. Permanent monitoring of Gulf Stream flow is now in place to track further changes.

53) Richard Wood, Hadley Centre. *New Scientist*, April 15, 2006.

54) NASA geophysicist Jeanne Sauber and geologist Bruce Molnia of the US Geological Survey suggest there may be a link between dramatic sea level rise and increased seismic activity. *New Scientist*, June 27, 2006. The theory is that as the weight of the water is redistributed around the globe, the continental shelves may rebound, increasing the occurrence of volcanic eruptions and earthquakes. There is no firm evidence that sea level rises to date have triggered such a process at this stage. The 2005 Asian tsunami was not caused by climate change.

CHAPTER 2
FEEDBACKS

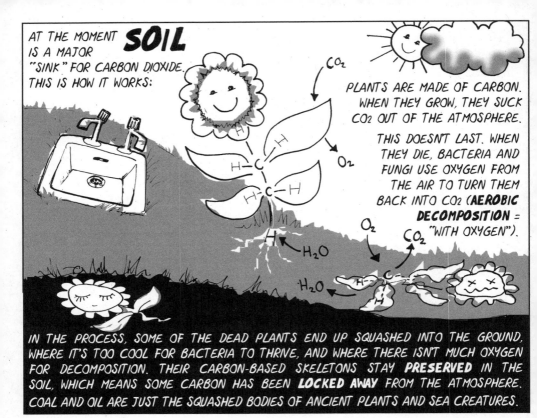

AT THE MOMENT **SOIL** IS A MAJOR "SINK" FOR CARBON DIOXIDE. THIS IS HOW IT WORKS:

CO_2

O_2

H_2O

PLANTS ARE MADE OF CARBON. WHEN THEY GROW, THEY SUCK CO_2 OUT OF THE ATMOSPHERE.

THIS DOESN'T LAST. WHEN THEY DIE, BACTERIA AND FUNGI USE OXYGEN FROM THE AIR TO TURN THEM BACK INTO CO_2 (**AEROBIC DECOMPOSITION** = "WITH OXYGEN").

O_2

CO_2

H_2O

IN THE PROCESS, SOME OF THE DEAD PLANTS END UP SQUASHED INTO THE GROUND, WHERE IT'S TOO COOL FOR BACTERIA TO THRIVE, AND WHERE THERE ISN'T MUCH OXYGEN FOR DECOMPOSITION. THEIR CARBON-BASED SKELETONS STAY **PRESERVED** IN THE SOIL, WHICH MEANS SOME CARBON HAS BEEN **LOCKED** AWAY FROM THE ATMOSPHERE. COAL AND OIL ARE JUST THE SQUASHED BODIES OF ANCIENT PLANTS AND SEA CREATURES.

SOME SOILS ARE PARTICULARLY GOOD CARBON SINKS: DEAD PLANTS IN WATERLOGGED **PEAT BOGS** CAN'T AEROBICALLY DECOMPOSE.

VERY UNLUCKY IRON AGE MAN, STILL WEARING A LEATHER BANGLE.

YIKES!

THERE'S A BIT OF **ANAEROBIC DECOMPOSITION**, WHERE PLANTS BREAK DOWN INTO **METHANE**, BUT GENERALLY, THE DEAD PLANTS (OR ANIMALS, OR PEOPLE!) WHO FALL IN THERE STAY ALMOST PERFECTLY PRESERVED.

AND **PERMAFROST** PREVENTS THINGS FROM DECOMPOSING IN EXACTLY THE SAME WAY THAT A FREEZER DOES.

It's freezing! I preferred Hawaii.

PEAS

CHICKEN -TYPE NUGGETS

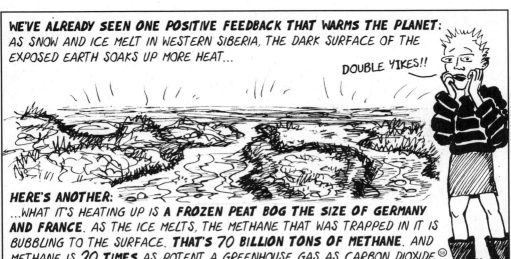

WE'VE ALREADY SEEN ONE POSITIVE FEEDBACK THAT WARMS THE PLANET: AS SNOW AND ICE MELT IN WESTERN SIBERIA, THE DARK SURFACE OF THE EXPOSED EARTH SOAKS UP MORE HEAT...

DOUBLE YIKES!!

HERE'S ANOTHER:
...WHAT IT'S HEATING UP IS **A FROZEN PEAT BOG THE SIZE OF GERMANY AND FRANCE.** AS THE ICE MELTS, THE METHANE THAT WAS TRAPPED IN IT IS BUBBLING TO THE SURFACE. **THAT'S 70 BILLION TONS OF METHANE.** AND METHANE IS **20 TIMES** AS POTENT A GREENHOUSE GAS AS CARBON DIOXIDE.[58]

AND HERE'S A THIRD: AS COLD EARTH AROUND THE WORLD BECOMES WARMER, PLANTS IN IT START DECOMPOSING FASTER. SINCE 1978, SOIL IN THE UK HAS GIVEN OFF **13 MILLION TONS OF CARBON DIOXIDE**...[59]

BURP

...WHICH NEATLY CANCELS OUT THE 12.7 MILLION TONS OF CO₂ WE'VE "SAVED" THROUGH ENERGY EFFICIENCY MEASURES IN THE SAME PERIOD.

THERE'S A LOT MORE DEAD PLANT MATTER STILL IN THERE, READY TO DECOMPOSE IN A WARMER WORLD. WHEN WILL WE REACH THE POINT WHERE SOILS START **PRODUCING** MORE CO₂ THAN THEY **ABSORB**?

Ooh, goody, another calculation... hmm, er... yes, got it... 2040

[60]

This is complete **poo.**

No, actually it's mud. It does look the same, but it smells quite different.

THE **OCEANS** ARE ANOTHER MAJOR SINK FOR CO₂ EMISSIONS...

CARBON DIOXIDE DISSOLVES INTO THE OCEANS

AND STRONG DEEP CURRENTS BRING MINERAL NUTRIENTS TO THE SURFACE

WHERE THEY FEED MICROSCOPIC PHYTOPLANKTON

WHICH IN TURN FEED JUST ABOUT EVERYTHING ELSE IN THE SEA.

WHEN THE PLANKTON DIE, THEIR BODIES BECOME BURIED IN THE SOFT SEDIMENT ON THE SEA BED, LOCKING AWAY CARBON FROM THE ATMOSPHERE...

...UNLESS IT STARTS GETTING WARMER

Lovely.

AND THE HOT LAYERS OF CARBON-DIOXIDE RICH WATER STRATIFY AT THE TOP OF THE OCEAN.

WHILE THE DEEP OCEAN CURRENTS SLOW DOWN

WITHOUT THIS VITAL MIXING OF COLD WATER NUTRIENTS, LIFE IN THE OCEANS GRINDS TO A HALT.

IN 2005, THE NORTHWEST PACIFIC WENT INTO ECOLOGICAL MELTDOWN. FREAK WEATHER PATTERNS (REMEMBER THOSE?) MEANT THAT COASTAL WATERS WARMED BY 7°C...

...PLANKTON LEVELS CRASHED BY 75%

AND SEABIRDS WASHED UP DEAD OF STARVATION ALL ALONG THE COAST. [62]

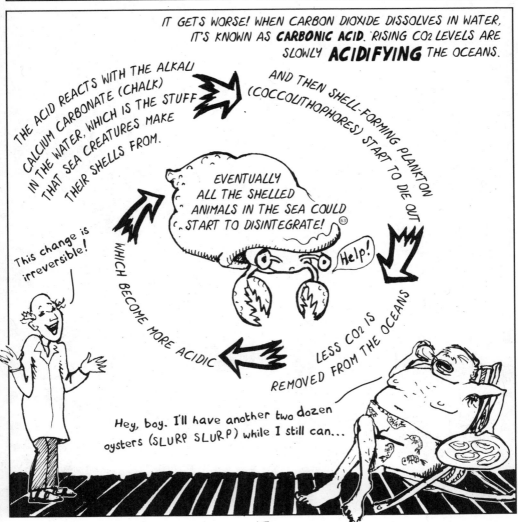

IT GETS WORSE! WHEN CARBON DIOXIDE DISSOLVES IN WATER, IT'S KNOWN AS **CARBONIC ACID**. RISING CO_2 LEVELS ARE SLOWLY **ACIDIFYING** THE OCEANS.

THE ACID REACTS WITH THE ALKALI CALCIUM CARBONATE (CHALK) IN THE WATER, WHICH IS THE STUFF THAT SEA CREATURES MAKE THEIR SHELLS FROM.

AND THEN SHELL-FORMING PLANKTON (COCCOLITHOPHORES) START TO DIE OUT

EVENTUALLY ALL THE SHELLED ANIMALS IN THE SEA COULD START TO DISINTEGRATE! [63]

Help!

This change is irreversible!

WHICH BECOME MORE ACIDIC

LESS CO_2 IS REMOVED FROM THE OCEANS

Hey, boy. I'll have another two dozen oysters (SLURP SLURP) while I still can...

AND IT COULD GET **REALLY REALLY BAD**. JUST AS A COLD CAN OF FIZZY DRINK RETAINS A LOT MORE CO_2 "FIZZ" THAN A WARM ONE, CARBON DIOXIDE COULD START **BUBBLING OUT** OF THE OCEANS IN A WARMER WORLD...

AHAH! BEHOLD THE TRIUMPH OF CAPITALISM OVER NATURE!

I HAVE TRANSFORMED THE SEAS INTO COCA-COLA!!!

There is a LOT more CO_2 contained in the sea than there is in the atmosphere. So this would be, er, the "mother" of all feedbacks. That is to say, rather large.

But still, this is a speculative model. I mean, we can't actually prove it will happen.

Until it has.

Er, yes.

64

48

Why do you have to be so negative? All this extra CO₂ is bound to be good for us in some way.

Plants love carbon dioxide. Trees will grow extra fast and soak up all the emissions.

I think you're wrong.

And why is that?

Well, you've been wrong about everything else in this book so far.

TREES DON'T "SOAK UP" CARBON DIOXIDE. THEY ONLY **STORE** CARBON UNTIL THEY DIE, WHEN THEY ROT, OR BURN, AND IT RETURNS TO THE ATMOSPHERE. **SO IF WE WANT TREES TO HELP LOWER OUR CARBON EMISSIONS**...

...WE HAVE TO STOP CUTTING THEM DOWN.

What's this book printed on anyway? Mmm, dead trees.

ALSO, PLANTS NEED MORE THAN JUST CO₂ TO GROW, THEY NEED **MOISTURE** AND **NUTRIENTS** FROM THE SOIL, WHICH ARE IN LIMITED SUPPLY. SO IN THE LONG RUN **MORE CO₂ DOESN'T MAKE TREES GROW FASTER**

EXCEPT FOR THE **AMAZON RAINFOREST**. IT IS SO **LUSH** AND **COMPLEX** THAT IT DOES HAVE THE ABILITY TO **ABSORB EXTRA CO_2** FROM THE ATMOSPHERE. AT THE MOMENT, THE AMAZON COMPENSATES FOR ABOUT 3/4 OF THE WORLD'S [66] CAR POLLUTION.

THE AMAZON CREATES ITS OWN CLIMATE...

THE DEEP ROOTS OF THE TREES TAP INTO UNDERGROUND STORES OF WATER,

WHICH EVAPORATE FROM THE LEAVES INTO CLOUDS

AND FALL AGAIN AS RAIN.

That'd be why it's called a rainforest then.

ONCE TEMPERATURES RISE A BIT MORE, AND SLIGHTLY LESS RAIN FALLS, ONLY A RELATIVELY SMALL NUMBER OF TREES HAVE TO DIE FOR **THE FOREST TO SUDDENLY LOSE THE ABILITY TO CREATE CLOUDS**...

THE RAINFOREST DIES. SO MUCH CO_2 IS RELEASED INTO THE AIR THAT GLOBAL WARMING SPEEDS UP BY 50% [67]

This is a speculative model, right?

Let me put it this way. We only need three years of drought to make this happen. There was a major drought in 2005, and another in 2006...

SCIENTISTS KNOW A LOT ABOUT CARBON DIOXIDE. **METHANE** IS MORE DIFFICULT TO TRACK. BECAUSE IT'S EMITTED BY A WIDE RANGE OF NATURAL SOURCES, MOST SCIENTISTS HAVENT INCLUDED IT IN THEIR MODELS....

We're not measuring THAT.

PARP

...AND MOST PREDICTIONS OF FUTURE TEMPERATURE RISES DONT INCLUDE THE POSSIBILITY OF **MASSIVE RELEASES OF METHANE**

AT THE MOMENT, THERE ARE 180 GIGATONS OF CARBON DIOXIDE IN THE ATMOSPHERE...

BUT **10,000** GIGATONS [68] OF METHANE ARE STORED UNDERNEATH THE SEA BED, IN THE FORM OF **METHANE HYDRATES**. THIS IS A WEIRD METHANE "ICE CREAM" WHICH IS STABLE AT **HIGH PRESSURE** AND **LOW TEMPERATURE**.

So either the oceans warm up, and the methane bubbles out

Or, once the weight of the melted Greenland and Antarctic ice sheets has gone, rising continents release the pressure, and the methane bubbles out.

But you're just speculating that this'll happen, right?

No. We know it's happened before.

SCIENTISTS CAN TELL US A LOT ABOUT PAST CHANGES IN THE EARTH'S CLIMATE. BY STUDYING THE CO_2 CONCENTRATIONS IN TINY BUBBLES OF AIR FROZEN DEEP IN THE ANTARCTIC ICE, THEY CAN TELL PRECISELY HOW WARM THE WORLD HAS BEEN FOR THE PAST 740,000 YEARS.[21]

Wow! 6°C global temperature rise in 20 years.[22]

THERE HAVE BEEN COLD SPELLS (ICE AGES) AND WARM SPELLS, AND **SURPRISINGLY**, WHEN THE CLIMATE SWITCHED BETWEEN THEM, IT DID SO VERY **RAPIDLY**.

SCIENTISTS CAN'T TELL US EXACTLY WHAT'S GOING TO HAPPEN IN THE FUTURE, BECAUSE LIVING PROCESSES ARE INFINITELY MORE COMPLEX THAN MODELS...

EEK! It's **ALIVE**!!

BUT WE DO KNOW THAT WE'RE POTENTIALLY MAKING THE EARTH **HOTTER THAN IT'S EVER BEEN**. AND IT'S LIKELY THAT IT WON'T BE A GRADUAL, EASY CHANGE TO A WARMER WORLD. INSTEAD, ONCE A CERTAIN THRESHOLD HAS BEEN REACHED, WE'LL HIT A **TIPPING POINT**; CLIMATE CHANGE WILL START TO **FEED ITSELF** AND **SPIRAL OUT OF CONTROL**...

Stop panic-mongering. The edge of that cliff is miles away.

IT'S LIKE WE'RE WALKING TOWARD THE EDGE OF A CLIFF. AT THE MOMENT, WE HAVE A CHANCE TO STEP BACK, AND THE CLIMATE WILL STABILIZE.

BUT ONCE WE'VE STEPPED OVER THE EDGE THERE'S NO GOING BACK

DON'T WORRY! WE HAVE THE **FRAMEWORK CONVENTION ON CLIMATE CHANGE.** COUNTRIES FROM AROUND THE WORLD HAVE SIGNED UP TO PREVENT **"DANGEROUS ANTHROPOGENIC** ← *"man-made"* **INTERFERENCE WITH THE CLIMATE SYSTEM."** IT'S JUST THAT **NO ONE SEEMS TO AGREE** ON QUITE WHAT THIS MEANS. WE'VE CAUSED **0.8°C** OF WARMING SO FAR. **IS THAT DANGEROUS ENOUGH TO TAKE ACTION?**

Yes

Yes

Yes

Yes

Obviously YES.

Yes

NO NO NO NO NO

I **REALLY** don't think so.

WELL THEN, **HOW MUCH MORE GLOBAL WARMING CAN WE GET AWAY WITH?**

How about another 2°C? ⑦ It's a nice round number, and, er, it probably won't trigger the really nasty runaway feedbacks.

Probably won't trigger the feedbacks. (Great.

Ha. Another 2°C. That'll take ages. I'll go and buy me a new air-conditioning unit and a nice big SUV.

HANG ON A MINUTE. **THE EARTH TAKES A LONG TIME TO WARM UP.** WE'LL ONLY **START** TO SEE THE EFFECT OF TODAY'S EMISSIONS IN 40 YEARS. AND IT TAKES **A THOUSAND YEARS** FOR THE OCEANS TO WARM UP FULLY. **IF WE WAIT** FOR IT TO GET 2°C WARMER, THEN **IT'LL BE TOO LATE.** WE'LL ALREADY BE **COMMITTED** TO MUCH MORE.

RIGHT NOW THERE'S ENOUGH GREENHOUSE GAS IN THE ATMOSPHERE TO CAUSE ANOTHER 0.8°C OF WARMING. [74]

IF WE ALL STOPPED EMITTING GREENHOUSE GASES TODAY, THEN THE WORLD WOULD STILL WARM UP AS MUCH AS IT ALREADY HAS, ALL OVER AGAIN.

SO WHAT TIMEFRAME ARE WE TALKING ABOUT FOR THIS 2°C RISE?

We could go with the European Union's target of limiting warming to 2°C between now and 2050?

NO! No! It'll KEEP GETTING WARMER AFTER THAT!

OK, 2°C IN 44 YEARS. NOW LET'S WORK OUT

WHAT LEVEL OF CARBON DIOXIDE WILL CAUSE THIS AMOUNT OF WARMING? [75]

Oh, if you *must* talk about capping CO_2, the European Union has worked this out. We're allowed carbon dioxide levels of 550 parts per million.
Twice pre-industrial levels.

I can hang onto these shares for a while.

THE EUROPEAN UNION HAS GOT ITS SUMS WRONG. [76] IF YOU TAKE **ALL THE PREDICTIONS** FROM **ALL THE MODELS,** AND **AVERAGE** THEM:

AT **550**ppm THERE'S A **75%** CHANCE THAT WARMING WILL EXCEED 2°C.

AT **450**ppm THERE'S STILL A **50–50 CHANCE OF ARMAGEDDON.**

BUT IF WE LIMIT CO_2 CONCENTRATIONS TO **400**ppm THEN THERE'S **ONLY A 25% CHANCE OF (EXTREMELY) DANGEROUS CLIMATE CHANGE.** WHICH IS BETTER ODDS.

AT THE MOMENT, CO_2 LEVELS ARE NEARLY AT 380ppm. **WE'LL HAVE TO ACT FAST.**

THERE'S ONE MORE CALCULATION THAT WE HAVE TO DO.

HOW MUCH CO_2 CAN WE EMIT AND **STILL MEET THAT** **400**ppm CEILING?

THE SOILS, SEAS AND FORESTS ARE GETTING PROGRESSIVELY **WORSE** AT **ABSORBING** OUR CARBON DIOXIDE POLLUTION, SO WE HAVE TO TAKE THAT INTO ACCOUNT.

Oh goody. More number crunching. At the moment we emit 7 gigatons a year... this really needs to fall to 2.8 gigatons a year... [77]

That means we need a 60% cut in global emissions by 2030.

And if there are 8.2 billion people in the world in 2030 that means we'll be allowed 0.33 tons of carbon each.

THE AVERAGE UK CITIZEN BURNS 3 TONS OF CARBON [78] A YEAR, SO

WE HAVE TO LEARN TO LIVE ON A TENTH OF THE AMOUNT OF FOSSIL FUELS THAT WE CURRENTLY USE.

IF WE HAVE THE **WILL**, THEN WE HAVE **ENOUGH TIME** TO MAKE THE CHANGES. **JUST**.

I think my head's going to explode. Can I read all that all over again?

You know, I'm really not convinced.

IF WE IGNORE THE SITUATION AND CO2 LEVELS RISE TO **DOUBLE** PRE-INDUSTRIAL LEVELS **THEN THE EARTH COULD WARM BY BETWEEN 6°C AND 10°C BY THE END OF THE CENTURY.**[79] THIS IS COMPLETELY OUTSIDE HUMAN EXPERIENCE. WE SIMPLY **DON'T KNOW** HOW BAD THIS WILL GET.[80]

MAYBE, AFTER ALL THE **RUNAWAY FEEDBACKS** HAVE RUN THEIR COURSE, AFTER THE FAMINES, AND THE FLOODS, AND THE EARTHQUAKES, AND THE TSUNAMIS, MAYBE **THE CLIMATE WILL STABILIZE AGAIN**, AT SOME UNKNOWN LEVEL, AND THE SURVIVORS WILL PICK UP THE PIECES AND CARRY ON.

Our stupid bloody ancestors. They did all this because they loved shopping?

OR, **WE COULD END UP LIKE VENUS**, WHERE 96% OF THE **CARBON** HAS BEEN CONVERTED TO ATMOSPHERIC CO2, AND THE SURFACE TEMPERATURE IS 420°C

IT'S POSSIBLE.

WE COULD BE TALKING ABOUT THE END OF LIFE ON EARTH.

55) Carbon dioxide measurements. Mauna Loa Observatory, www.mlo.noaa.gov. This graph is an artistic representation.

56) "Global Warming to Speed Up as Carbon Levels Show Sharp Rise," *The Independent on Sunday*, January 15, 2006.

57) Carbon sinks and emissions from B. Hare and M. Meinhausen, *PIK Report 93*, Potsdam Institute for Climate Impact Research, 2004, reproduced in Colin Forrest, *The Cutting Edge: Climate Science to April 2005*. Campaign Against Climate Change, http://portal.campaignccc.org/files/THE_CUTTING_EDGE_CLIMATE_SCIENCE_TO_APRIL_05.pdf.

58) "Climate Warning as Siberia Melts," *New Scientist*, August 11, 2005.

59) "Vicious Circle of Emissions Is Speeding Up Climate Change," *The Independent*, September 8, 2005; "Soil May Spoil UK's Climate Efforts," *New Scientist*, September 7, 2005. See also M. Torn et al, Lawrence Berkeley National Laboratory, who have factored the increase in soil emissions of CO2 into their climate models and found that estimates of temperature rise by 3000 should be revised upwards to 7.7°C. *Geophysical Research Letters*, reported in *The Guardian*, May 23, 2006.

60) Peter Cox and Chris Jones, Hadley Centre.

61) Jef Huisman et al, University of Amsterdam, published in *Nature*. *The Independent*, January 19, 2006.

62) "Fish Numbers Plummet in Warming Pacific," *The Independent on Sunday*, November 13, 2005.

63) John Raven, University of Dundee, report commissioned by the Royal Society, reported in "Marine Crisis Looms Over Acidifying Oceans," *New Scientist*, June 30, 2005.

64) CO2 solubility is basic physics.

65) Ram Oren et al, Duke University, found that increasing CO2 levels stimulated trees to grow faster for about 3 years, but after this they reverted to normal rates of growth. *New Scientist*, May 23, 2001.

66) Mark Maslin, *Global Warming: Causes, Effects, and the Future* (Voyageur, 2002).

67) Peter Cox, Hadley Centre, *New Scientist*, November 22, 2003.

68) Mark Maslin, *Global Warming*.

69) The role of methane hydrates in the end-Permian extinctions is explored by paleontologist Michael J. Benton, *When Life Nearly Died: The Greatest Mass Extinction of All Time* (Thames and Hudson, 2003). See also George Monbiot, "Shadow of Extinction," *The Guardian*, July 1, 2003 and Mark Maslin (by email) re "... the Palaeocene-Eocene Thermal Maximum (PETM) extinction, a short intense period of global warming about 55 million years ago when a huge amount of methane burped out of the ocean causing run-away global warming. An extra 5° degrees C was added to an already very very warm world. It took about 100,000 years for that extra carbon to be removed from the atmosphere."

70) The Storegga Slide, a massive methane-hydrate-induced tsunami, inundated the Shetland Isles with 20 meters of water 7080 years ago, wiping out settlements of Mesolithic people along the Scottish coast. *New Scientist*, August 4, 1990.

71) "Record Ice Core Gives Fair Forecast," *New Scientist*, June 9, 2004.

72) Fred Pearce, "Doomsday Scenario," *New Scientist*, November 22, 2003. Verified by Mark Maslin.

73) A 2°C rise by 2150 is proposed in "Stabilising Climate to Avoid Dangerous Climate Change: A Summary of Relevant Research at the Hadley Centre," January 2005. A rise of 2°C seems to be a common unofficial "best guess" among future climate scenarios for limiting global warming, although the time frames for projected rise vary.

74) "Scientific Results from the Hadley Centre 2002" contains the calculation that as of 2002 levels of greenhouses gases have committed the earth to 1.1°C of warming by 2100, and 1.6°C of warming overall, relative to pre-industrial times. I have subtracted the 0.8°C of warming that has already occurred from the 1.6°C long-term overall figure.

75) Just to make it all extra confusing, some climate calculations talk about carbon dioxide levels and some consider the warming effect of all greenhouse gases, expressed as the equivalent of CO2 — "CO2 equivalent." I am talking about straight carbon dioxide here, and ignoring the other warming gases.

76) Calculations by Malte Meinshausen, Swiss Federal Institute of Technology, Zurich. *New Scientist*, February 3, 2005.

77) These calculations are from Colin Forrest, *The Cutting Edge: Climate Science to April 2005*.

78) There are two sets of figures regarding personal emissions, too. Some authorities talk about metric tons of carbon dioxide emitted, which is heavier (the weight of the extra oxygen molecules). To convert carbon to carbon dioxide, multiply by 44, then divide by 12.

79) These figures greatly exceed the predictions of the 2001 IPCC report. They are from three leading climatologists — Meinrat Andreae, Max Planck Institute for Chemistry, and Peter Cox and Chris Jones, Hadley Centre. The predictions are based on an analysis of the temporary cooling effect of aerosols currently in the atmosphere. If these are greater than previously estimated, then the warming effect when they disperse will be more severe. The study combines this assessment of aerosol cooling effect with an analysis of the effect of the natural carbon cycle (reduced uptake of CO2 from trees, soils and oceans) to arrive at the higher figure. *Nature*, June 30, 2005, reported in *New Scientist*, June 29, 2005.

80) In discussing the consequence of a temperature rise greater than 6°C, Meinrat Andreae (see above) commented, "It is so far outside the range covered by our experience and scientific understanding that we cannot with any confidence predict the consequences for the Earth."

CHAPTER 3
WHAT ARE WE DOING?

ALL THE ENERGY IN THE WORLD COMES FROM THE SUN

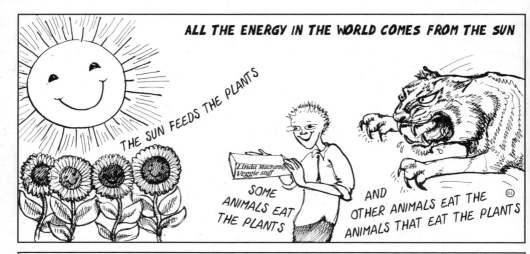

THE SUN FEEDS THE PLANTS

SOME ANIMALS EAT THE PLANTS

AND OTHER ANIMALS EAT THE ANIMALS THAT EAT THE PLANTS

AND WE GOT ALL OUR ENERGY FROM SUN-FED PLANTS AND ANIMALS, UNTIL WE STRUCK, FIRST COAL...

...AND THEN OIL.

The first commercial oil well was drilled in Pennsylvania in 1859.

The first coal-fired steam railway opened in northern England in 1821.

FOSSIL FUELS ARE MADE FROM THE BODIES OF PLANTS AND ANIMALS THAT GREW, IN THE SUN, OVER MILLIONS AND MILLIONS AND MILLIONS OF YEARS. SO, REALLY, **OIL IS COMPRESSED SUNSHINE.** AN INCREDIBLY **LARGE AMOUNT** OF SUNSHINE.

WE'VE FOUND A WAY OF CASHING IN ON A WHOLE PLANET'S WORTH OF **STORED-UP SOLAR ENERGY**, AND NOW WE'RE BENT ON **BURNING IT ALL**, ALL AT ONCE.

OIL IS AMAZING

YOU CAN MAKE FLAMMABLE LIQUID **FUELS** FROM IT, WHICH CAN BE EASILY STORED, TRANSPORTED AND DISPENSED.

YOU CAN MAKE THICK, HEAVY **TAR** FROM IT.

AND YOU CAN MAKE LIGHTWEIGHT, WATERPROOF **PLASTIC** FROM IT, THAT CAN BE EASILY MOLDED AND COLORED AND STORED.

WHICH MEANS.

YOU CAN MAKE BARBIE DOLLS.
YOU CAN MAKE DUCT TAPE
YOU CAN MAKE TUPPERWARE
YOU CAN MAKE PVC UNDERWEAR
YOU CAN MAKE PLANES FLY
YOU CAN MAKE HIGHWAYS
YOU CAN MOVE MOUNTAINS
AND WHAT ELSE CAN YOU MAKE?
A QUICK BUCK

BECAUSE OIL IS SO **USEFUL**, IT IS INCREDIBLY **PROFITABLE**. WHICH MEANS THAT OIL-PRODUCING COMPANIES AND NATIONS ARE INCREDIBLY **RICH**, AND **POWERFUL**. AND THEY USE THAT POWER TO **CARRY ON GETTING RICHER**, BY **ENCOURAGING** OUR TENDENCY TO **USE**, AND TO **WASTE**, **MORE AND MORE OIL**.

1936
A mass-transit system based on trains and streetcars was definitely more efficient... But let's face it, I'll make more money if everyone drives around in their own, individual, two-ton metal box.

Oil and car companies bought up and dismantled electric rail networks in 45 American cities between 1932 and 1956.

2006
I bought an extra-large car so I could see over all the other cars on the road.

Everyone else was buying extra-large cars, and I couldn't see over the top of them any more. So now I commute to work in this!

WE'RE BURNING A **MILLION YEARS'** WORTH OF STORED SOLAR ENERGY, **EVERY YEAR**. THIS **INCREDIBLE OIL BONANZA** HAS BEEN A LOT OF **FUN**, BUT IT'S **NOT EXACTLY SENSIBLE**.

OIL COMPANIES DON'T REALLY RUN THE WORLD.

WE *LIVE* IN A DEMOCRACY.

AND THE INTERNATIONAL COMMUNITY **HAS** MADE AN EFFORT TO ADDRESS THE PROBLEM OF CLIMATE CHANGE. IN 1992, THE **UNITED NATIONS FRAMEWORK CONVENTION ON CLIMATE CHANGE** WAS CREATED, AND IN 1997, INDUSTRIALIZED NATIONS SIGNED UP TO

THE KYOTO PROTOCOL.

THEY AGREED TO **FREEZE EMISSIONS** AT 1990 LEVELS, AND THEN TO **REDUCE** THE RATE AT WHICH WE'RE EMITTING GREENHOUSE GASES BY A WHOPPING **5.4%** BY 2010. IT'S TAKEN NEARLY **TEN YEARS** FOR ENOUGH COUNTRIES TO RATIFY IT FOR IT TO ACTUALLY BECOME LEGALLY BINDING, BUT STILL, **IT'S A START**.

Of course, these reductions have to be made in the most cost-effective manner possible.
Let's start a market for countries to trade their carbon pollution.
(That way, I can get fabulously wealthy by gambling on trading in future emissions quotas.)[85]

Hmm. I'm suddenly suspicious.

There's no need for *us* to cut down our oil consumption when we can *buy* carbon credits from abroad.
Russia's well under quota. Toss 'em a few dollars and it's businesski-as-usual for us.

So the Russian economy's in recession. How come that means you can *increase* your emissions?
Where does the environment benefit?

Ooh! ooh! I know another way to get round it.[86] We can plant trees in the Third World.
But as the world heats up, those carbon "sink" forests will die from heat stress. I'm not sure we're really getting to grips with the problem here.

KYOTO WAS AN OPPORTUNITY FOR WORLD LEADERS TO GET TOGETHER AND MAKE A REAL DIFFERENCE TO THE FUTURE OF THE PLANET. **IT *LOOKS* LIKE THAT OPPORTUNITY'S BEEN WASTED.**

hee hee

THE PROTOCOL DOESN'T COVER **AVIATION EMISSIONS**, WHICH ARE GROWING SO FAST THAT THEY THREATEN TO CANCEL OUT EVERYTHING THE PROTOCOL HAS ACHIEVED.[87]

BRITAIN'S CARBON DIOXIDE EMISSIONS HAVE **INCREASED** BY 9% SINCE 1990.

10 OUT OF 15 EUROPEAN NATIONS ARE **NOT GOING TO MEET THEIR REDUCTIONS COMMITMENTS**.

AND THAT INCLUDES PORTUGAL AND IRELAND, WHO WERE ALLOWED SMALL INCREASES. [88]

NOW GERMANY'S **STALLED** ON REDUCING INDUSTRIAL POLLUTION ANY FURTHER. [89]

CANADA'S WRITTEN OFF ITS TARGETS AS "UNACHIEVABLE." [90]

AUSTRALIA'S **REFUSED TO RATIFY IT**. AND THEY CAN BE SURE THEY WONT BE SUBJECT TO INTERNATIONAL SANCTIONS, BECAUSE SO HAS **THE WORLD'S MOST POLLUTING NATION...**

*You know, for a comic book, this is **NOT VERY** CHEERFUL!*

KICK KICK KICK

63

THE US GOVERNMENT HAS RENOUNCED THE KYOTO PROTOCOL AND REFUSES TO TAKE PART IN ANY NEGOTIATIONS WHICH WOULD LEAD TO NEW, BINDING COMMITMENTS. [92]

AMERICA EXPECTS THE RATE AT WHICH IT PUMPS OUT CO_2 TO INCREASE BY MORE THAN A THIRD BY 2025. [93]

WHY ARE THEY OCCUPYING IRAQ, ONE OF THE 3 MOST OIL-RICH COUNTRIES IN THE WORLD? WHICH BEGS THE QUESTION,

THE US HAS CRITICIZED THE KYOTO PROTOCOL AS **UNFAIR**, BECAUSE IT **ONLY** REQUIRES **INDUSTRIALIZED COUNTRIES** TO CUT THEIR EMISSIONS.

Ah'm not puttin' none of MAH pie back 'nless y'all put YOURS back too!

INDUSTRIALIZED COUNTRIES HAVE **CAUSED** THE CLIMATE CHANGE, AND **PROFITED** FROM THE EMISSIONS, SO IT'S ONLY FAIR THAT THEY SHOULD **LEAD THE WAY** IN SOLVING THE SITUATION. STILL, **EMISSIONS FROM THE MAJORITY WORLD ARE RISING TOO**, IN SOME CASES, **ALARMINGLY**.

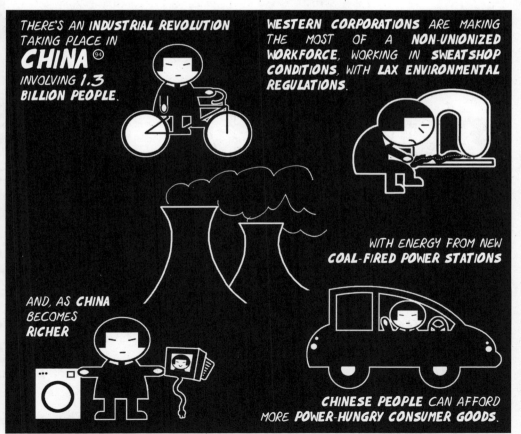

THERE'S AN **INDUSTRIAL REVOLUTION** TAKING PLACE IN **CHINA** [94] INVOLVING **1.3 BILLION PEOPLE**.

WESTERN CORPORATIONS ARE MAKING THE MOST OF A **NON-UNIONIZED WORKFORCE**, WORKING IN **SWEATSHOP CONDITIONS**, WITH **LAX ENVIRONMENTAL REGULATIONS**.

WITH ENERGY FROM NEW **COAL-FIRED POWER STATIONS**

AND, AS **CHINA** BECOMES **RICHER**

CHINESE PEOPLE CAN AFFORD MORE **POWER-HUNGRY CONSUMER GOODS**.

WHILE WESTERN NATIONS ARE UNWILLING TO MEET THEIR LIMITED KYOTO COMMITMENTS, WHERE IS THE INCENTIVE FOR OTHER COUNTRIES TO CURB FOSSIL-FUEL USE?

I'm in the money! The International Energy Outlook is rosy.[95] By 2030, oil production will increase to 118 million barrels a day.

But that's really bad.

Hmm, and it's also, er, fundamentally incorrect.

We probably don't have enough oil for that kind of growth.

WHAT?!!

NOT ENOUGH OIL???

They haven't got very much oil?

Oil is a finite resource. There's only a certain amount of it in the ground, and it's rather unclear exactly how much.

CRASH!!

Under OPEC rules, the more oil a country has, the more it's allowed to sell. That's a strong incentive for a nation to pretend to have more than it does. So, it kind of looks like everyone's lying about how much they've got left.

I'll take a guess that there are 2 trillion[96] barrels left. That's only enough for another 70 years at *present rates* of consumption.

Oil...run...out.
But it **CAN'T** run out! I **NEED** it.
I *need* it for all the *planes* and the *trucks* and the *ships* that take all the *things* halfway round the world to sell! And for the *tractors* to grow *food*, and the *fertilizers* to douse it with, and the *plastic* to package it in, and for all the *cars* to drive to the *cute little drive-thru restaurants...*

I *NEED* IT FOR THE *POWER STATIONS*
I *NEED* IT FOR EXOTIC FOREIGN *HOLIDAYS*
I *NEED* ECONOMIC *GROWTH!*
I *NEED* **PROFITABLE** RETURNS!
I **NEED** THAT CHEAP ENERGY!
DON'T YOU SEE?
I HAVE A **RESPONSIBILITY** TO MY **SHAREHOLDERS!!!**

Oh, you don't have to worry about oil running out. No, the real problem will come much sooner than that. Once we've burnt *half* the oil in the world, then the trouble begins!

THAT'S WHEN WE HIT **PEAK OIL**

[97] FROM THAT POINT ON, THERE IS **LESS AND LESS OIL AVAILABLE** TO FUEL THE DRIVE FOR **CONTINUED ECONOMIC EXPANSION**. AND THE OIL THAT IS LEFT IS THE STUFF THAT IS **HARDER** TO DRILL OUT, AND **MORE EXPENSIVE** TO OBTAIN.

The world economy, er, can't keep growing without cheap, abundant oil. And the stockmarkets that feed off it are, um, vulnerable to collapse. It looks like we're headed for an absolutely stupendous global recession.

So that'll be all right then. There won't be any oil to burn, and the climate will be saved.

WAIL

SOB SOB

Uh, no. We can easily burn enough fossil fuels for CO_2 concentrations to double, or triple, or even quadruple. We'll still get the horrendous runaway warming, but the economy will nosedive at the same time. That's why we need to invest in alternative technologies now, while we still can...

Great! Now we're *both* really depressed.

THUMP THUMP THUMP

So, it looks like we have to switch to a low-carbon economy.

There's still plenty of coal. We can burn more coal. We can make diesel fuel by liquefying coal.

All is not lost.

No, 'cause, if we stop using fossil fuels now, we'll still have enough money to develop alternatives. We could be the technological leaders in the post-carbon world.

You can get oil from shale-tar sands. It takes two tons of sand to get one barrel of oil, but we can do it. [98]

Listen. Oh, no, never mind.

You're a maniac and we're all going to fry.

THERE IS AN URGENT NEED FOR US TO REDUCE OUR DEPENDENCY ON FOSSIL FUELS. BUT IT'S SUCH A BIG PROBLEM, IT SOMETIMES SEEMS EASIEST TO IGNORE IT.

A SHOE! A SHOE! Oh don't be ridiculous. It's simply a large ridged, brown patch of sky. Perfectly natural. Nothing to worry about.

IT'S ALSO A LONG-TERM PROBLEM - THE EFFECTS OF OUR ACTIONS TODAY WON'T BE FELT UNTIL MANY YEARS HAVE PASSED. AND OUR SOCIETY IS OBSESSED WITH NEW, TRIVIAL, SHORT-TERM EVENTS AND POLICIES.

THIS IS WHAT TODAY'S NEWS WOULD LOOK LIKE IF EVERYONE WAS CONFRONTING THE MOST IMPORTANT ISSUE IN THE WORLD...

...The Government today announced plans to decommission three of the runways at Heathrow airport, with the aim of establishing a new mega-orchard at the sit

CLIMATE CHANGE IS STILL REALLY BAD

MADONNA EMBARKS ON WORLD TOUR ON DONKEY BACK: POPE OUTRAGED

"This is taking religious allegories too far!"

WHEELS we road test the urban bike everyone's talking about

Jeremy Clarkson "nearly rehabilitated" Troubled star to be considered for release back into the community

Inside the Beckhams' garden: Posh Spice shows us her vegetable patch!

a stick of celery | Victoria Beckham

As Shell and BP cease trading, we ask, is there any future for oil companies?

ACME WIND GENERATORS FEEL THE RAW THROBBING POWER

BUT WE AREN'T...

...Hey, climate change is very very bad...

...and peak oil's coming...

...We have to change our lives...

HE END OF THE WORLD IS NIGH

No one cares.

They just think I've gone Enviro Mental.

AND OIL USE IS SO INTERWOVEN INTO OUR LIVES THAT...

What can I do anyway?

...OPEN THE FRIDGE...

I'm just one person.

SWITCH ON A KETTLE...

Anything I do won't make any difference.

TURN ON THE TV...

Pathetically insignificant.

...AND YOU JUST MADE THE PROBLEM WORSE.

81) Richard Heinberg, *The Party's Over: Oil, War and the Fate of Industrial Societies*, 12-14.
82) *The Party's Over*, 50-53. On a small scale, humans have used oil and coal for heating and lighting for at least 4,000 years. By the 17th century, coal had become essential to the English economy, and large-scale coal mining had begun. However, with the development of coal-fired railways, the coal-powered industrial revolution really picked up steam.
83) *The Party's Over*, 66.
84) Center for Responsible Politics. www. opensecrets.org.
85) "Since carbon credits are tradable instruments with a transparent price, financial investors have started buying them for pure trading purposes. This market is expected to grow substantially, with banks, brokers, funds, arbitrageurs and private traders eventually participating. Emissions Trading PLC, for example, was floated on the London Stock Exchange's AiM market in 2005 with the specific remit of investing in emissions instruments." Emissions trading entry, www.wikipedia.org.

There are several emissions trading markets in existence. The text here refers to a global market in which First World countries buy credits from poorer nations. This means that a kind of carbon colonialism occurs, where richer countries buy up the easiest, cheapest options for reducing emissions abroad. Come the time when Majority World countries try to reduce their own emissions, the cheapest options will also have been snapped up.

There are also internal carbon markets, such as the one set up by the European Union. For example, 12,000 European power plants and industrial sites have been issued with permits to pollute, which they can only trade among themselves. This system is more egalitarian and should help markets systematically reduce their carbon budgets. Unfortunately, jockeying for quotas by national governments resulted in an overall allowance for carbon emissions that *exceeded* the amount actually being burned. So as a tool for reducing emissions, the scheme has initially been astoundingly ineffective. "Governments Accused of Giving Industries Permission to Pollute," *The Guardian*, May 16, 2005.

86) The term "Third World" is used ironically here. "Majority World" is preferable, as it gives a more accurate impression of the proportion of the world that is impoverished.
87) John Vidal, "Adding Fuel to the Fire," *The Guardian*, June 30, 2006.
88) "Europeans Missing Their Kyoto Targets," *The Independent*, December 27, 2005.
89) "Germany Slams Brakes on Emissions Targets," *New Scientist*, June 6, 2006.
90) "Canada May Be Caving In on Kyoto," *New Scientist*, May 27, 2006.
91) George Bush Sr. said this before the 1992 Rio Earth Summit.
92) For an account of the US administration's attempts to actively scupper climate negotiations, see "America's War with Itself" by George Monbiot, *The Guardian*, December 21, 2004.
93) The US Energy Information Administration projects an increase of 30 to 47% between 2000 and 2025. "Record US Greenhouse Gas Emissions in 2004," *New Scientist*, December 21, 2005.
94) "Forget the Threat of Terrorism: China Is About to Flick the Switch on a Global Energy Crisis and a Time Bomb that Will Bring Massive Destruction Worldwide," *The Sunday Herald*, July 25, 2004.
95) Energy Information Administration, "World Oil Markets," *International Energy Outlook 2006*.
96) Kenneth Deffeyes, geophysicist at Princeton University, estimates the remaining world oil reserves at 2.013 trillion barrels. Hubbert's Curve, www.wikipedia.org.
97) Attempts to predict exactly when peak oil will hit are frustrated by the secrecy that surrounds remaining oil reserves. Kenneth Deffeyes reckons it has already passed, in 2004. Geophysicist Colin Campbell gives 2010 as a likely date. The Association for the Study of Peak Oil gives 2006-2015 as the years in which it is most likely to occur. The peak will only be detectable retrospectively; a period of fluctuating prices at the peak itself will be followed by a steady year-on-year price climb. See *The Party's Over*, Chapter 3, for an analysis of peak oil predictions and naysayers.
98) *The Party's Over*, Chapter 4, gives an analysis of the energy return over energy invested in oil substitutes.

CHAPTER 4

WHAT ARE WE GOING TO DO?

"WHATEVER YOU DO WILL BE INSIGNIFICANT. IT IS VERY IMPORTANT THAT YOU DO IT."

MAHATMA GANDHI

Climate change is a very big problem, which means...

BLINK

...it's a very big **CHALLENGE IN DISGUISE!**

BOING!

It's here!

CRAX

It's not going to go away!

And so am I**! AND...**

I-can-either-spend-the-rest-of-my-life-ignoring-the-situation-and-dooming-the-human-race-to-inexorable-self-destruction

?

OR! I can **FACE UP TO IT!**

and **WORK OUT**

exactly what **I CAN DO** to make it **BETTER**.

STARTING WITH BREAKFAST:

Insanesbury's* supermarket trucks its food halfway round the world, then three times round the country before it gets to your plate.

Instead, we're eating seasonal food from a local farm veg-box scheme, and wholefoods from a food co-op.

And we've gone veggie. We don't need cows farting methane for our food.

Is that Insanesbury's home delivery? I want snow peas from Venezuela, and I want them now.

INSANESBURYS
WE'RE EVERYWHERE.
TRY TO AVOID US
BET YOU CANT.

INSANESBURYS
LOW-PRICE
CRISPIES

*SAINSBURY'S IS A LARGE SUPERMARKET CHAIN.

72

IN EUROPE, HOUSES EMIT MORE CO2 THAN VEHICLES DO.

So, I'm insulating the walls and attic, draft-proofing, adding heavy curtains, reflectors behind the radiators, and blocking off the chimney when it's not being used. (99)

a giraffe draft stopper

And I'm going to turn down the thermostat, and wear a thermal vest.

You wait and see, this is going to be the height of fashion.

BRITISH HOMES USED TO BE HEATED TO 13°C, NOW IT'S MORE LIKE 21°C, AND THAT'S ONLY BECAUSE WE WEAR FLIMSY SUMMER CLOTHES ALL YEAR ROUND.

Appliances on standby waste **4 MILLION** tons of CO2. (100)

Doing nothing!

FLICK

It doesn't cost anything to switch to a green energy supplier. (101)

Wanna save money? Buy less new stuff!

Recycling your waste is great, but reducing it and re-using things is even more important.

We did buy some low-energy lightbulbs, though. These are going to save a ton of CO2.

why d'you need to leave a light on in an empty room?

FLICK

We've moved into a bigger place. Heated pool. Yeah, fantastic.

NOW FOR SOME LIFESTYLE CHANGES

Let's try using public transport.

BUS STOP

I think I can identify why this isn't an incredibly popular option.

BUS STOP

BRITISH PUBLIC TRANSPORT IS THE MOST EXPENSIVE IN THE WORLD. UNFORTUNATELY, THAT DOESN'T MEAN THAT IT'S EXTENSIVE, REGULAR OR RELIABLE![102]

WITH THE EXCEPTION OF AIR TRAVEL.

Of course, most important, we have to stop flying.

WHAT? Not FLY? But Fryin Air is doing a special deal, fly to Malaga for 75p!

IT'S NOT JUST THE FACT THAT **AIRCRAFT BURN VAST AMOUNTS OF UNTAXED FOSSIL FUELS**. AIRPLANES ALSO LEAVE TRAILS OF **ICE CRYSTALS** IN THE SENSITIVE **UPPER ATMOSPHERE**, WHICH **DIRECTLY** ACT TO **HEAT UP THE PLANET**. THE **TOTAL WARMING EFFECT** OF AIR TRAVEL IS **THREE TIMES** GREATER THAN THE CO_2 EMISSIONS.

Air traffic is the single fastest-growing cause of climate change. And passenger numbers are set to double by 2030. Which is going to destroy any attempt to reduce UK CO_2 emissions.[103]

But all my friends are going!

If individuals don't start taking responsibility for avoiding air travel right now, then we are All Going To Be In Big Trouble.

I wanted to go to Spain with my friends

Then you can go on the bus.

(sulk)

74

But the Climate Cuddles ™ website says that if I send them some money, they can offset the emissions from my flight.

And you believe them?

Well, I want to.

A RETURN FLIGHT FROM LONDON TO MALAGA GENERATES 0.25 TONS OF CO_2. ADD IN THE WARMING EFFECT OF THE VAPOR TRAILS, AND THAT'S THE EQUIVALENT OF **THREE QUARTERS OF A TON OF CO_2**.

CLIMATE CUDDLES WILL TAKE YOUR MONEY AND SPEND IT ON SOME LOW-ENERGY LIGHTING. **OVER THEIR LIFETIME**, THREE LIGHTBULBS **WILL** SAVE THAT CO_2, **BUT THEY'LL TAKE FIVE YEARS TO DO IT**.

AND IN THE MEANTIME, WHILE EVERYONE KEEPS ON FLYING, THOSE POSITIVE FEEDBACKS ARE STARTING TO KICK IN...

...THE CLIMATE IS EDGING TOWARD THAT TERRIBLE TIPPING POINT...

Hmm, suddenly the bus looks cheaper.

YOU CAN'T RELEASE A WEDGE OF CO_2 IN TWO HOURS, TODAY, AND PRETEND YOU'VE "OFFSET" IT BY SAVING ENERGY IN FIVE, TEN OR FIFTY YEARS' TIME. THAT KIND OF BEHAVIOR WILL MEAN THAT IN FIFTY YEARS' TIME, WE WON'T HAVE A PLANET FIT TO LIVE ON.

TO BE **SAFE**, A CARBON OFFSET SCHEME NEEDS TO SAVE CARBON DIOXIDE IN THE **SAME TIME FRAME** AS IT IS EMITTED. WANNA TRY **SAVING 3/4 TON** OF CO_2 IN **TWO HOURS**? MAYBE YOU COULD **BUY 70,000 LOW-ENERGY LIGHTBULBS**, AND MAKE SURE EACH ONE REPLACES A CONVENTIONAL BULB? [104]

What do you say – we'll jet over to New York, Maurice can do your hair, then we'll fly back for Ascot...

OI! NO! You're going to WIPE OUT all my CO2 savings, just so your girlfriend can get her HAIR CUT!

Oh do calm down. The scientific expert chaps are bound to come up with a solution. Let's leave it to the experts, eh? Admit it, they've got the brains, and you've got the beauty.

Explain that carbon sequestration plan again... [105]

Um, first, we capture the CO2 from fossil-fueled power stations.

SOLVENT

COTTON WOOL

Ah yes, and then what do we do with it?

We could inject it into saline aquifers, 800 meters underground. Or sink it deep into the ocean bed, where it would solidify into hydrates.

No, no, there was a better idea.

Er, we could pump it into disused coal mines and siphon off methane for use as a fuel...

...Or we could use it to flush out oil fields. It makes the oil runnier, so it's easier to pump out the dregs. And about 3/4 of the CO2 stays in the ground.

But methane is a greenhouse gas!

COAL

That's the one! I like that one! We'll do that one!

But you have to be sure that that CO2's going to stay locked away for the next thousand years. [106] Wouldn't it be safer to just *not produce it* in the first place?

Now tell me about hydrogen fuel cells. They've got marketing potential.

It's quite simple. Combine hydrogen, oxygen from air, and a catalyst...

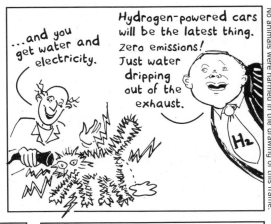

...and you get water and electricity.

Hydrogen-powered cars will be the latest thing. Zero emissions! Just water dripping out of the exhaust.

Hydrogen's not very easy to store. It's bulky, it's flammable, and it makes steel brittle and liable to shatter.

And, er, more important, hydrogen isn't actually a fuel. I mean, it takes more energy to make hydrogen than it produces when you burn it. So it doesn't make energy. It just *stores* it. [107]

I know that.

You could get it from water by electrolysis, using the power from a massive wind farm.

I could. But it's much cheaper to make hydrogen from natural gas.

Hey. Natural gas is a fossil fuel!

Ha ha. They think it's green! I know it's not! [108]

The big money's in climate change these days.

Change the company logo to a sunflower.

Arrange a photo opportunity - me in a kaftan with the Dalai Lama.

Never fear! The solution is here! Bring me uranium! Enrich it with its radioactive isotope 235! Build me power stations! Encase them in supersafe containment structures!*

And let it all go **CRITICAL**...

Now my whites are so white that they glow! Nuclear power saves 98% of CO_2, when compared to ordinary, coal-fired power stations.**[109]

A ton of enriched uranium produces 75,000 times as much energy as a ton of coal. [110]

Yo! Pump it into the grid!

JUST CALL ME DADDY.

*THE REACTOR AT CHERNOBYL DIDN'T HAVE ONE OF THESE. MODERN DESIGNS OF NUCLEAR POWER STATIONS ARE SAFER.
** TAKING INTO ACCOUNT THE FOSSIL FUELS USED IN MINING THE URANIUM AND BUILDING THE POWER STATION, **BUT**, CRUCIALLY, NOT THE DECOMMISSIONING PROCESS.

And then what do you do with it?

Oh, I don't know. We'll worry about that later.

There have been nuclear power stations for 50 years now. Each one makes a thousand tons of toxic waste a year. Uranium mines make far more. ⑪

That's all going to stay radioactive for the next **TEN THOUSAND YEARS**.⑫

How do you store something safely for ten thousand years?

On a poverty-stricken planet that's prone to hurricanes and floods?

Factor that into your costings, and it won't look like such a profitable enterprise.

And where's the uranium going to come from?

There's only 50 years' worth of assured supplies, ⑬ and none of that's in the UK.

Oh good. We wouldn't want uranium miners. They'd be a terrible drain on the health service.

AND, if this is the answer to the energy crisis, is it OK for every country in the world to go nuclear?

Once you can enrich uranium, you can make nuclear weapons.

I thought we were trying to save the world, not blow it to pieces.

People think it's impossible. People think there's nothing we can do. But that's just because we're so used to living an energy-intensive lifestyle that we can't imagine it any other way.

Once you find out what the alternatives are, and start using them, they become real, and it all becomes possible.

Take cars, for example. We love them. We think we need them. Shame. There just isn't any way that we can keep on using cars the way we do now.

Wanna run them on hydrogen? Looks like we'd need to double the capacity of the national grid to get enough electricity to make the fuel. [114]

Biofuels sound like a nice idea. We could make petrol from sugar beet, and veg-oil diesel from rapeseed, and the plants soak up as much CO_2 as they give out when they're burned. But where're we going to grow them? We'd need $4\frac{1}{2}$ times as much cropland to grow biodiesel as there is in the whole of the UK. [115]

So, we'll import it. Right now, people are starving in poorer countries, while their land is used to grow animal fodder so that we can eat roast beef. And next we're going to make them grow our gasoline and diesel? I don't think so.

We need to get on our bikes.

The self-propelled travel pod of the future. It triples the efficiency of the average human, and is 25 times more energy efficient than a car. [116] It requires no fuel, mechanics is a piece of cake, and it gets you fit! Unlike a car, where the more people use them, the slower they go, with a bike, the more you ride it, the faster you get.

This is a multi-purpose transportation unit, which is also suitable for heavy loads. Input solar energy in the form of plant-based fodder, and collect high-quality compost from the exhaust end. Capable of 20 times the sustained effort of a human being. Can be quite endearing apparently, although, personally, I think they smell funny.

OI! CUT ME UP WOULD U?

CAR FREE

Let's have cheap, regular, reliable public transport. And make it compatible with bicycles, so you can get the bus home with your bike if you need to. When trains are cheaper than cars, people will use them - there's nothing particularly pleasant about having to drive. But at the moment, cars are priced wrong. Once you've paid for insurance and car license, you feel like an idiot shelling out for public transport. If we transfer those costs onto gas at the pump, then we'll have an incentive to reduce car use.

Why don't we reorganize our towns? The planning system in this country is powerful and well organized. Easy. Analyze new building projects in terms of their carbon emissions, and only allow the most sustainable developments. We could reunite areas of work and housing, so we can walk to work. We'll have car-free streets and city centers. Housing co-ops could get 100% mortgages, and we'll see the rebirth of functioning communities.[117] With "passive house" building standards, new homes can heat themselves with sunshine.[118] The technology's there. We can just start using it.

As for the energy crisis. At the moment, we're *wasting* energy, and it's cooking the planet. Duh! The current energy debate is all about meeting projections of increased demand. But what's the point in keeping the lights on, when most of them aren't illuminating anything?

Centralized energy generation is criminally inefficient. The national grid wastes 2/3 of the energy that it generates.[119] So, we cut down the amount of power available on the national grid, and then people can start powering themselves.

Carbon rationing makes sense. When you restrict the electricity that's available, then people use it efficiently. You just don't leave the TV on standby if it means there won't be any power left to watch your favorite program later on.

If you want more power, then you'll get a wind generator, or a solar panel. And, for when it's neither windy nor sunny, a cycle generator. We're all going to have fantastically toned thighs.

The most energy-efficient businesses will be the new market leaders. Low-energy appliances will be in vogue. And we could grow biomass on urban spaces to power generators for hospitals and schools.

Oi, keep cycling, I'm nearly onto the next level.

GRAND THEFT PUSHBIKE

Hey, modern high-energy living isn't that great. Depression and obesity are endemic. We might just enjoy coming together for a common cause. And since we have to scale down our energy use at some point, the sooner we do it, the easier it's going to be.

In the war on climate change, we have two very powerful weapons for changing our habits. Television is a great way of conveying complicated information to millions of people.

WHY DON'T YOU *GET UP AND GO AND DO* **SOMETHING LESS BORING INSTEAD?**

And, we can reform the financial system. Most people, most of the time, base their decision-making on how much something costs. So, we tax high-carbon products, and subsidize low-carbon ones... Wow, suddenly people find it *really* easy to do the green thing.

SAVING THE WORLD

1) STOP BURNING FOSSIL FUELS

2) REFORM OUR SOCIETY SO WE ALL STOP BURNING FOSSIL FUELS

3) PERSUADE EVERY OTHER NATION IN THE WORLD TO STOP BURNING FOSSIL FUELS

Right then. Better get on with it.

Fortunately, here's an international framework for achieving just that, that someone drew up earlier.

CONTRACTION AND CONVERGENCE

CONTRACTION AND CONVERGENCE IS BASED ON THE IDEA THAT **EVERY PERSON** ON EARTH HAS AN **EQUAL** RIGHT TO POLLUTE IT, AND THAT **NONE** OF US HAS A RIGHT TO **JEOPARDIZE** OUR FUTURE EXISTENCE.

ALL THE COUNTRIES GET TOGETHER. WE AGREE ON A **SAFE LIMIT** FOR GREENHOUSE GASES. THEN WE **CONTRACT** OUR EMISSIONS YEAR BY YEAR, UNTIL WE ALL **CONVERGE** AT THE TARGET.

EVERYONE IN THE WORLD ENDS UP WITH THE **SAME CARBON ALLOWANCE**. IF YOU DON'T USE IT ALL, YOU CAN **TRADE** THE EXTRA.

I sold my extra allowance to the Americans, and now I can afford to send my daughters to school.

I really wanted to fly to Australia. It cost me thousands of pounds in carbon credits, but that's OK.

I'll treasure this lemon-fresh facial towel forever.

That's cool. Poor, low-emitting countries gradually get richer. And rich, high-emitting countries have to pay fully for their lifestyles. Wicked, that's sorted. Now we just have to persuade the politicians.

What you're proposing isn't economically viable. Ludicrous! Impossible! We *must* have unfettered access to fossil fuels. It's a basic prerequisite for economic growth!

I dunno, what's so fantastic about that? I mean, war, drugs, crime and disasters can all be good for the economy, but terrible for people who suffer from them.

Planned obsolescence is great for economic growth, but it means that everything you buy falls apart after six months.

We could invent new indicators for how well our country is doing. We could have a happiness index, instead of an economic indicator of progress. [121]

We have to stop viewing our whole planet as something we can parcel up and sell, because once we've sold it all, we'll have nothing left.

We don't have to. We don't need economic growth.

Wash your mouth out with soap and water, young lady.

Do you want someone to tell you that you'll make more money out of stopping burning fossil fuels than you will out of burning them. Is that the only reasoning that you're prepared to listen to?

Ooh, ooh, tell me more!

The world economy is growing at 3% a year. The cost of dealing with natural disasters is growing by 10% a year. At this rate, by 2065, the entire gross domestic product of the world will be spent mopping up catastrophic climate chaos. [122]

Anyway, you don't have to have this conversation with me. You can have it with the climate.

What you're proposing isn't economically viable. Ludicrous! Impossible!

LOOK INSIDE YOURSELF

SOMEWHERE, THERE'S AN IDEALISTIC CHILD, READY TO GET OUTRAGED AT WHAT EVERYONE ELSE IS DOING

THIS IS YOU

THIS IS YOU

DEEP IN THERE, THE SCIENTIFIC ANALYST IS FASCINATED, ENTHRALLED BY THE SHEER SIZE OF THE PROBLEM THAT WE FACE

BUT WE ALL LOVE THE LUXURY AND CONVENIENCE THAT FOSSIL FUELS BRING TO OUR LIVES. WE'RE ALL LAZY. WE'RE ALL GREEDY. WE COMPROMISE THIS PLANET BY OUR VERY EXISTENCE.

AND THIS IS YOU

IT'S TIME TO TAKE CONTROL OF OUR FATE

99) Check federal and state/provincial websites to find out which grants are available for home insulation in your area.

100) George Monbiot, "Thanks, But We Still Don't Need It," *The Guardian*, June 11, 2006.

101) This statement is slightly misleading. Subscribing to a renewable energy tariff is currently slightly more expensive than buying fossil fuel and nuclear-derived electricity. However, it doesn't actually cost anything to switch supplier.

102) George Monbiot, "Goodbye Carmageddon," *The Guardian*, September 15, 1999.

103) "Everyone's Carbon Dioxide Emissions Must Go to Zero to Allow for Aviation Pollution Reveals Major Analysis of UK Climate Change Targets," media release, Tyndall Centre, September 21, 2005.

104) Duncan Law, letter to *The Independent*, April 3, 2006. Carbon offset firms can underestimate the warming effects of flights by calculating emissions per seat (airplanes have an average occupancy of 80%), and by using a lower multiple for the warming effect than the 2.7 that I have used.

105) "Clean Energy Special: Going Underground," *New Scientist*, September 3, 2005, and "Deep Sea Graveyard for CO2," *New Scientist*, August 8, 2006.

106) It takes 1,000 years for the planet to fully heat up; therefore CO2 must be locked away for many thousands of years to not contribute to anthropogenic warming. Large-scale leaks of CO2 from underground stores could suffocate people and animals.

107) *The Party's Over*, 146-9.

108) Reforming natural gas or coal into hydrogen and using it in a fuel cell results in fewer greenhouse gas emissions than if the fossil fuels are burned directly. So the technology is green — maybe only light green — but still green (*The Party's Over*, 147). However, oil companies are currently advertising hydrogen-powered initiatives as "zero emission," which is also misleading. Currently, hydrogen is commercially produced almost entirely from fossil fuels. Hydrogen is an inefficient and problematic solution to the forthcoming energy crisis. See also James Howard Kunstler, *The Long Emergency: Surviving the Converging Catastrophes of the Twenty-first Century* (Atlantic Monthly Press, 2005).

109) "4.4 tC/GWh [nuclear], compared to 24tC/GWh for coal and 97tC/GWh for gas." Sustainable Development Commission, *The Role of Nuclear Power in a Low Carbon Economy*, March 2006, 5.

110) Figures from the UK Department of Trade and Industry. George Monbiot, "Thanks, But We Still Don't Need It," *The Guardian*, August 20, 2006.

111) *The Party's Over*. Each nuclear power station is also responsible for the annual production of 100,000 metric tons of radioactive uranium tailings from the mining process.

112) The US Environmental Protection Standards estimates that after 10,000 years, spent nuclear fuel will no longer pose a threat to public health and safety.

113) Demand for uranium-235 may start to outstrip supply as early as 2020. "Human Health May Be the Cost of a Nuclear Future," *New Scientist*, June 10, 2006. See also Michael Meacher, "On the Road to Ruin," *The Guardian*, June 7, 2006. Fast-breeder reactors use uranium-238, which is far more abundant than uranium-235. However, these reactors create plutonium, which is extremely hazardous and can be used for nuclear weapons. There is currently only one fast-breeder reactor in operation. www.wikipedia.org.

114) Based on US figures for car use and electricity production. George Monbiot, "A Different Kind of Revolution," *The Guardian*, April 26, 2005.

115) George Monbiot, "Feeding Cars, Not People," *The Guardian*, November 23, 2004. See also Monbiot, "Worse Than Fossil Fuel," *The Guardian*, December 6, 2005. Biofuels are not carbon neutral, as fossil fuels are used intensively in agricultural production. Recycled vegetable oil can be regarded as a truly green alternative to diesel, but there is only enough spare chip fat to fuel 1/380th of the current UK fleet of vehicles.

116) "The conventional bicycle is among the most efficient means of human locomotion. To travel one kilometer by bike requires approximately 5 to 15 watt/hours (w/h) of energy, while the same distance requires 15 to 20 w/h by foot, 30 to 40 w/h by train, and over 400 in a singly occupied car." Justin Lemire-Elmore, "The Energy Cost of Electric and Human-Powered Bicycles," 2. www.ebikes.ca/sustainability.

117) Sounds far-fetched? The government used to issue favorable-rate 100% mortgages for housing co-ops until Margaret Thatcher abolished the scheme in 1979. Promotion of housing co-ops would solve both the energy inefficiency and the social isolation suffered by single-parent and single-occupier households.

118) The Passive House, or Passivhaus, is a German design where the insulation and draft-proofing are of such a high standard that the house can heat itself by passive solar gain. They are being constructed across Germany and Austria for as little as 8% above conventional construction costs.

119) Greenpeace advertisement, "The Energy Review (Facts Included)," *The Independent*, June 21, 2006.

120) Contraction and Convergence was formulated by Aubrey Meyer and is promoted by the Global Commons Institute (www.gci.org.uk). Under C + C carbon trading still occurs, but unlike with the Kyoto Protocol, every country in the world is obliged to reduce their fossil fuel use. This prevents "carbon colonialism," where rich nations cherrypick the cheap carbon offset deals from the Majority World. Instead, all nations institute their own indigenous carbon-reduction programs, and surplus capacity is traded for a fair price.

121) The New Economics Foundation is conducting research into using a "happiness index" as an indicator for national progress.

122) Study by Munich Re, the world's largest reinsurance firm, quoted by Dr. Andrew Dlugolecki, chairman of the UNEP Insurance Industry Initiative, www.saka-consul.com/Mita/dr_ad.html.

TAKE ACTION:

www.climatecrisis.net Website for Al Gore's documentary, *An Inconvenient Truth*.

www.greenpeace.org Coordinated media-friendly direct action through regional groups, and cybercampaigning that you can do at home.

www.pollutionprobe.org Canadian environmental organization that presses for green power and sponsors Clean Air Commute week.

www.davidsuzuki.org Website for the David Suzuki Foundation. Includes suggestions on how to go carbon neutral.

KEEP UP WITH CLIMATE CHANGES:

www.climatewire.org Website detailing climate-related news summaries from around the world.

www.climatechangenews.org Similar, but better. Essential articles are highlighted to save you from information overload.

www.ipcc.ch The Intergovernmental Panel on Climate Change publishes its assessment reports online.

www.realclimate.org Climate science by climate scientists. Interesting online comment and debate.

The Ecologist Available at bookstores or online at **www.theecologist.org**. Investigative journalism on environmental issues. Their 1999 climate issue was the inspiration for the first 16-page version of *Weird Weather*.

New Scientist Available at bookstores or online at **www.newscientist.com**. Includes comprehensive coverage of climate science.

INTERACTIVE ONLINE GAMES:

Greena the Worrier Princess presents a fun introduction to the issues at **www.abc.net.au/science/planetslayer/** Very silly.

Also check out the *Climate Challenge* on-line computer game, which can be played at **www.bbc.co.uk/sn/hottopics/climate-change/climate_challenge/**

RECOMMENDED FURTHER READING:

Bruges, James. **The Little Earth Book**. The Disinformation Company, 2004. Succinct, fascinating account of current financial and social structures, and their alternatives.

Dauncey, Guy with Patrick Mazza. **Stormy Weather: 101 Solutions to Global Climate Change**. New Society/Tandem Books, 2001. Packed with practical suggestions.

Dow, Kirsten and Thomas E. Downing. **The Atlas of Climate Change: Mapping the World's Greatest Challenge**. University of California Press, 2006. Maps the impact of climate change around the world. A pictorial assessment of the global situation.

Flannery, Tim. **The Weather Makers: How Man Is Changing the Climate and What It Means for Life on Earth**. Harper Collins/Atlantic Monthly Press, 2006. Readable and authoritative overview by acclaimed Australian scientist and writer.

Gelbspan, Ross. **Boiling Point: How Politicians, Big Oil and Coal, Journalists and Activists Are Fueling the Climate Crisis — and What We Can Do to Avert Disaster**. Basic Books, 2004. Reveals how fossil fuel industries have directed US domestic and foreign policies, together with a roadmap for economic adjustment to climate change.

Godrej, Dinyar. **The No-Nonsense Guide to Climate Change**. New Internationalist/Between the Lines/Verso Books, 2001. Interesting introduction to the subject, with good Majority World perspectives.

Heinberg, Richard. **The Party's Over: Oil, War and the Fate of Industrial Societies**. New Society, 2003. Thorough analytical explanation of peak oil and the forthcoming energy shortfall.

Hillman, Mayer. **How We Can Save the Planet**. Penguin/Putnam, 2006. Dense, fact-filled overview of climate change, and solutions for the UK, including carbon rationing.

Lynas, Mark. **High Tide: The Truth About Our Climate Crisis**. Picador, 2003. Gives a personal account of current climate crises.

Lynas, Mark. **Six Degrees: Our Future on a Hotter Planet**. Fourth Estate, 2007. Explores what's in store if we don't sort it out.

Maslin, Mark. **Global Warming: A Very Short Introduction**. Oxford, 2004. Comprehensive and readable, with a thoughtful analysis of the arguments of climate change "sceptics."

McCarthy, Donnachadh. **Saving the Earth Without Costing the Earth: 500 Simple Steps to a Greener Lifestyle**. Fusion, 2004. Provides help with auditing your environmental impact and plenty of ideas for improvement.

McDonagh, Martine. **I Have Waited, and You Have Come**. Myriad, 2006. Novel set in a climate-changed future. It's really good, and I'm not just saying that because we share a UK publisher.

Monbiot, George. **Heat: How to Stop the Planet from Burning**. Doubleday Canada/South End Press, 2006/2007. Explores ways and means to make a 90 percent cut in CO2 emissions by 2030 a reality.

Pearce, Fred. **The Last Generation: How Nature Will Take Her Revenge for Climate Change**. Corgi, 2006. Punchy, pacy book with a thorough exploration of positive feedback mechanisms.

HOW MUCH CARBON DIOXIDE DO YOU EMIT IN A YEAR?

The first thing you can do to take action on climate change is to calculate your carbon footprint. There are a number of websites that will help you do this, but here are two:

www.epa.gov/climatechange/ emissions/ind_calculator/html
www.safeclimate.net/calculator

Now you can compare yourself with the international standard. The average US citizen emits 19,730 kg of CO_2 per year. The average Canadian emits 17,240 kg of CO_2 each year. * If you're doing better than that, don't feel too smug. Start working on getting it down to 2,500 kg of CO_2 per year. Yikes. And that's still twice what we'll be allowed in 2030, if there are 8.2 billion people by then. Double yikes. This is a radical lifestyle change. We need root and branch reform to be able to meet it. Still, calculating your emissions will give you an idea of which areas of your life are most energy hungry, and help you to see how to change them.

Set realistic targets. Tackle some of the big figures like flying and commuting. Low-carbon living will help you to see how we need to change our society to save our world.

* Emissions figures are taken from OECD in Figures 2006–2007, which is available for dowload at www.oecdobserver.org/news/ fullstory.php/aid/1988/OECD_in_Figures_ 2006-2007.html

METRIC CONVERSION CHART

Temperature
1 Celsius degree is equivalent to 1.8 Fahrenheit degrees.

To convert temperature from Celsius to Fahrenheit:
$$^{\circ}F = (^{\circ}C \times 1.8) + 32$$

To convert temperature from Fahrenheit to Celsius:
$$^{\circ}C = (^{\circ}F - 32) / 1.8$$

Length
1 centimeter = .04 inches
1 meter = 3.28 feet
1 kilometer = 3,280 feet

Area
1 hectare = 10,000 square meters = .01 square kilometers = 107,640 square feet = 2.47 acres

Weight
1 kilogram = 2.2 pounds
1 metric ton* = 1,000 kilograms
1 gigaton = 1 billion metric tons

* In this book, a **ton** refers to a metric ton (tonne).
* Should you need to work out what weight of CO_2 results when a given amount of carbon is burned, multiply by 44, then divide by 12.

INDEX

ABOUT THE AUTHOR

KATE EVANS IS A CARTOONIST AND ENVIRONMENTALIST WHO CURRENTLY LIVES IN A HEDGE JUST OUTSIDE BATH. SHE SPENDS HER TIME ALTERNATELY WORRYING ABOUT THE STATE OF THE PLANET AND CONTRIBUTING TO THE OVER-POPULATION PROBLEM.

THE PRODUCTION OF THIS BOOK WAS PREDOMINATELY POWERED BY A SOLAR PANEL AND A 350-WATT WIND GENERATOR. IT WAS HEATED BY A WOOD-BURNING STOVE, PASSIVE SOLAR HEATING, AND THE WEARING OF SKIING SALOPETTES. GIVE THAT WOMAN A BLUE PETER BADGE.

THIS BOOK WAS WRITTEN, RESEARCHED, ILLUSTRATED AND LAID OUT BY KATE EVANS. SHE HAS PREVIOUSLY WRITTEN (RESEARCHED, ILLUSTRATED, LAID OUT AND PUBLISHED) COPSE: THE CARTOON BOOK OF TREE PROTESTING ABOUT HER EXPERIENCES AS AN ENVIRONMENTAL ACTIVIST. THE FOOD OF LOVE – BREASTFEEDING YOUR BABY IS NEXT, PROBABLY FOLLOWED BY SOMETHING ON PREGNANCY AND BIRTH. SHE IS THE AUTHOR OF NUMEROUS STRIP CARTOONS AND FULL-LENGTH COMIC FEATURES INCLUDING WHAT'S REALLY GOING ON IN THERE? ABOUT FERTILITY AWARENESS, AND BIG BROTHER, AN EXPLORATION OF UK CIVIL LIBERTIES (SOMETIMES REALITY IS SCARIER THAN REALITY TV). MORE ON THE WEBSITE - CHECK IT OUT.

SHE CAN ALSO DO A MEAN ILLUSTRATED LECTURE ON CLIMATE CHANGE, IF YOU NEED SOMEONE TO BRIGHTEN UP YOUR DISCUSSIONS OF DOOM AND GLOOM.

www.funnyweather.org

MANY THANKS TO DONACH, DUNCAN LAW, GEORGE MARSHALL, MARK BROWN, GEORGE MONBIOT, FRED PEARCE, ANEETA, COLIN FORREST, CHRIS JONES, MARK MASLIN AND EVERYONE AT TIPPING POINT FOR ACADEMIC INPUT, CORINNE PEARLMAN AND CANDIDA LACEY FOR BELIEVING IN CARTOONS, CHARLES AND ELEANOR ANDERSON FOR LAUNDRY SERVICES, ROSIE EVANS AND ADAM MARSHALL FOR FINANCIAL SUPPORT, SHARON FOR CARING, MIKE HOLDERNESS FOR WEB GEEKERY, MIPSY FOR ARTISTIC INSPIRATION AND LOUDEN FOR BEING CUTE. APOLOGIES TO TONY AND SU. IF YOU'RE NOT ONE OF THE PEOPLE MENTIONED ABOVE, THAT WAS PROBABLY QUITE BORING. ANYWAY, GET IN TOUCH WITH ME AT kate@cartoonkate.co.uk AND TELL ME WHAT YOU THINK OF THE BOOK.

USE THIS BOOK TO CHANGE YOUR LIFE, BECAUSE WHAT HAPPENS NEXT, DEPENDS ON WHAT YOU DO NOW...